WE ARE ONE

A MANIFESTO FOR HUMANITY

Simenon Honoré

Published by
Spirit of the Rainbow™
P. O. Box 483, Tunbridge Wells, Kent, TN2 9QU

If you would like to order further copies of this book,
or wish to contact us please write to:
Spirit of the Rainbow
P. O. Box 483
Tunbridge Wells
TN2 9QU
United Kingdom

Or visit our website at: **www.spiritoftherainbow.org**

ISBN 978-0-9566767-0-2

Logo by Magenta Design & Print, Tunbridge Wells, TN4 9PH
Printed by CPI Antony Rowe, Chippenham and Eastbourne

In memory of

Lenin

for his genius and stupidity

in seeking to build

his vision of heaven on earth.

ACKNOWLEDGEMENTS

This book is based on over half a century's learning and experience, so inevitably many people have had an impact on what I have written. There have been great world teachers such as Omraam Mikhaël Aïvanhov and Mother Meera who have had a profound influence on me. Then there have been those like Peter Goldman and the team at the Centre of New Directions who have illuminated my journey through their wisdom and kindness. Others like Dr Maya Angelou have inspired me for having the courage to be all the colours of their rainbow. The great therapist and teacher Marianne Fry taught me so much about being fully human by her own example. Books like Milovan Djilas' *The Unperfect Society* and Helen Greaves' *Testimony of Light* have contributed to my thinking on the place of humankind in the universe. Historical figures like Lenin, Trotsky and that greatest of all revolutionaries, Joan of Arc, all have had important lessons for me. Hundreds of extraordinary ordinary people have touched my life in various ways and to these I owe a great debt.

For the writing of this book I would like to thank the monks and nuns of the Monastery of the Holy Trinity, Crawley Down, Sussex for providing such a beautiful setting in which to write the first draft of this work. Also Sara and Sybil Samson, Kay and Aaron Broadhouse, Bridget Mary-Clare, Pam Blake-Wilson, Ann Barter, Amanda Tidman, Phoebe de Larrabeiti, the Goring family, Simon Laurence, Diane Hedge, Ella Watt, Estari Powers and Matthew Clarke for their comments on my text. Thanks too to Tarquin Grossman and Helen West who very kindly typed up the first draft of the manuscript. A special thanks goes to the Tunbridge Wells Mental Health Resource: to Derek Springett, the Centre Co-ordinator, for his invaluable help in reading over the various drafts and being tirelessly supportive and encouraging. Also to Centre staff members Kate Mages, Claire Horwood, Claire Bartlett and Jane Manton for their help in preparing the manuscript. I am most grateful to John MacFarlane BSc (Hons) M.Inst.P. for checking over the scientific content of the manuscript and for his helpful suggestions. A special thanks to Patrick Houser for casting his astute editorial eye over the text and for his invaluable help in the preparation of the book for publication. I am more indebted than I can adequately express to my aunt Jasmine for her encouragement and support in the long years between writing this book and its publication. Thanks too to my mother for her contribution to the funding of this project.

Above all I wish to thank those members of the congregation of Jireh Chapel, Lewes, in East Sussex, without whose principled and resolute opposition to almost everything I believe in, I would never have understood the need to give the Oneness a voice in the writing of this book.

CONTENTS

PREFACE

In the summer of 1971 I went to Yugoslavia as an exchange student with my friend Misha Arsenijevic. We travelled from Dubrovnik on the Dalmatian coast across the mountains of Montenegro and then onwards to Belgrade. During this journey three incidents took place which were to give birth to the worldview that lies at the heart of this book.

The first occurred in a little church high up in the mountainous region of southern Serbia. It was here that I heard for the first time the Slavonic liturgy of the Serbian Orthodox Church. I had heard many beautiful church services before in the West, but there was something quite different about this. It had a profound simplicity to it, a sense of mystery and of holiness that resonated with something at first indefinable inside me, which I called "innerness". Later, I was to understand that I had been awakened to the presence of my soul. And so this feeling that had lain buried deep within me all my life now called to me. I have learnt that if I heed that calling I will be drawn to my highest destiny, such is its power. Many millions of people, I believe, have moments when they awaken to the presence of their soul, be it through a great crisis, a vision of beauty, a sense of stillness or a feeling of great love. For the soul will always seek to express itself as fully and freely as we humans will allow it.

The second incident was at Kragujevac, site of a terrible massacre during the Second World War. I remember being shown a schoolroom, exercise books open on the desks, work half-finished, as the children had been taken out mid-way through their lessons and shot. There had been a sickening, surreal orderliness to it all: rows of what looked at first glance like bicycle racks, with pairs of metal prongs protruding from concrete walls. But the prongs were too wide for cycle tyres and the real purpose became shockingly clear: they were for peoples' legs, so they could be all lined up, neatly in rows, to be executed. Thirty years later when I was telling this story to someone I realised that, without being consciously aware of it, I had made a decision then. At that grey, grim monument to inhumanity I had resolved to do all within my power to heal the terrible wounds humanity had inflicted on itself by working for the unity of the peoples of this planet.

The last incident took place in Belgrade. I was sitting outside in a street café, talking with Misha. We were midway through a very intellectual conversation about God, or the gods, when I became aware of an extraordinary sensation in and around me. I could sense a unifying presence binding me to Misha and to everything else. I was awakened to a subtle yet immensely powerful force that was almost a physical sensation at the tips of my fingers and yet it was something I could sense simultaneously within my own being. At the time I struggled to find the words to describe what was happening to me and I still do so today; for in the end there are no words for this. It is my hope, however, that by my telling my story, it may be possible for others to recognise what I experienced. For I believe I caught a glimpse of the great underlying truth of existence, *the oneness of all things*. And from that moment in a street in Belgrade oneness was no longer a theory, an abstract concept, a philosophical proposition. Now I knew, in every part of my being:

It is true, it is alive, it is real.
We are one.

Simenon Honoré
August 2010

INTRODUCTION

Throughout human history we have struggled to deal with the challenges that face us. For many, even today, it is the daily task of meeting the needs of our survival - finding enough to eat and drink, shelter, warmth and security. For others, the challenges are more subtle but no less real: coping with relationships, with work and not least with ourselves; trying to find meaning and purpose in our lives; making sense of the universe and our place in it - the list is endless. On a global level the last century has ushered in great movements for social and political change together with tremendous scientific and industrial developments. It has also witnessed humanity sink to unprecedented levels of warfare and genocide. Our powers of creativity and destruction have become awesome. We have even reached the point of supreme cleverness and folly where our technology enables us to destroy our planet many times over. We may ask ourselves how much as human beings we have really advanced at all. It is as if our intellects were in the 21st century but our hearts were still in the age of dinosaurs.

This book is a response to this situation we find ourselves in. It offers a vision of what humanity can achieve in building a new world based on the simple truth that we are one. For as a people we face the same destiny. A nuclear accident in one country creates a radioactive cloud that does not stop merely because it has reached the national borders of another. The effects of a volcanic eruption on the climate can be felt across the world. In our global economy a financial crisis in one country has repercussions everywhere. A rogue state developing weapons of mass destruction or sponsoring terrorism threatens everybody. For better or for worse we share a common humanity and what happens to one part of our planet will eventually affect all of it.

What I have written is based on my own experience of life. Coming from a European perspective inevitably there is a cultural bias. I cannot hope to understand what it is like to be an Indonesian factory worker or a doctor in Tanzania. What I do hope however is that what I write will find some resonance with people in different parts of the world so that we can recognise *a unity of purpose within a diversity of experience*. My own life, with its mix of a privileged background yet also being at times at the margins of society has perhaps given me a more rounded view than I might otherwise have had. I am also aware that my search for oneness has come out of a sense of profound separation from the world around me that I have had since I was a child. Looking back I can see that had it not been for this, I might never had begun my quest for a deeper sense of connection with the universe. And in giving voice to my sense of oneness through writing this book I also had to face its shadow: a sense of extreme isolation and alienation that I was called upon to revisit so that it might be healed. I believe that it is through being tested by such experiences that the principles we hold so dear come to have meaning in our lives.

The book explores the idea of oneness in a number of different ways. Part I explores the meaning of oneness both in a scientific and a spiritual sense. In dealing with the concept of oneness, I have found these two forms of understanding essentially complement each other like two languages describing the same phenomena. The idea of oneness is also contrasted with the prevailing ideology of "dualism", focusing on the events of 9/11, that brought these two worldviews together in one terrible moment. Drawing from its lessons, I have suggested how we might turn 9/11 into an opportunity for world healing. Part II sets out five broad principles within the overall theme of oneness that could help us tackle the key issues facing humanity. I have also included some ideas about how these principles might be put into practice. Finally Part III suggests ways in which we might become involved in the process of realising our sense of oneness on this planet.

During the course of this book I express a range of views on a wide variety of topics and people can choose for themselves those they find most useful to work with. In so doing I have used both intellect and intuition for I believe both are indispensable tools in our search for answers. But I make no claim to absolute truth. I do believe however that all the challenges we face, both personally and globally, have arisen in our lives in order to be healed. They are not there to punish us, or present us with insurmountable obstacles, or grind us into the dirt, and they are certainly not there to make victims of us. They are only there because they need to be healed and we, the people of this planet, have the resources to do it. Individually and collectively we have the power to build our own heaven on earth. There are six billion of us, together we can create a better world for ourselves and our future generations. If we align ourselves with the highest ideals, if we work to heal that which is hurt and damaged in all of us, if we are willing to be who we truly are, we can do it. We can do it just by our being. We have no idea how powerful we are. It is a great responsibility.

We can do something truly marvellous with our lives. All of us have the opportunity to participate in this great work. And for this we do not need to be a genius or millionaire. We just have to be willing to begin the work, starting with ourselves. For truly it is said:

"A journey of a thousand miles begins with a single step."

So I invite you to take that first step and turn the page.

PART I:

THE SENSE OF

ONENESS

THE SENSE OF ONENESS

From the moment the universe was created the sense of oneness was born. Billions of years of evolution have passed, yet it is still with us today. It is found within our physical makeup and our spiritual inheritance. It comes from the simple fact that everything that exists today comes from a single source, of which we are a part. We can see this in different ways: modern scientific theory tells us that at the birth of the cosmos, all matter was concentrated into a single incredibly dense point (or "singularity"). At the moment of Creation it exploded outwards and has been doing so ever since. Over time this material has evolved into an infinite variety of shapes and structures whether it be an asteroid, a plant, an animal or even the "dark matter" that seems to fill so much of the known universe. But we all ultimately come from the same component elements of matter and energy however different we may appear now.

It is essentially the same story if we look at the origins of the cosmos from a spiritual perspective. In a universe created by God all life including ourselves comes from this single Divine source and in essence remains part of its Creator for all eternity. There is no separation. Of course we all manifest in various ways. As humans we each have a different consciousness; we may argue amongst ourselves, even kill each other but nevertheless we are united at the deepest level in an all-embracing Divine Oneness. Either way we look at it we have always been and will always be part of the great oneness of all things. This is the great truth.

What has happened over time however is that we humans have begun to lose contact with this inner knowledge. Many of us have lost our sense of connection with the universe, with this planet, with each other, even with ourselves. Above all we have lost touch with the underlying oneness of all existence. We have often acted towards each other and the world around us as if we were entirely separate beings. We can damage the planet because we imagine we are somehow apart from nature. We can be indifferent to the suffering of others or perpetrate the most appalling acts of cruelty, because we cut ourselves off from the knowledge that these are our fellow human beings. We may think the universe is there just for us to exploit its riches without a thought for the consequences because we cannot see that we form part of an organic unity that makes up the cosmos.

Yet at the same time the movement for unity and planetary awareness across the world has never been stronger. People are coming together in all sorts of ways - self-help groups, co-operatives and spontaneous gatherings that coalesce to meet new challenges and opportunities. The planet is going through a healing crisis as the old order with all its apparent certainties breaks down. The sense of oneness is re-emerging. We are rediscovering the ancient wisdom that there is an underlying unity to all Creation. Our task now is to make good that sense of oneness.

Hand in hand with this process we can also respect our diversity as individuals and cultures. In this we hold two apparently contradictory truths: that we are all unique beings and that we form part of a single unity. Both statements are true but they are true at different levels. Both need to be honoured. At present we could say we are out of balance because in the course of our evolution we have lost the sense of our oneness and the feeling for that which binds us all together - our shared humanity.

EXPERIENCING ONENESS

Yet there is a journey we can take that can lead us to an experience of this unity. There are many pathways to reach this point but for now let us suppose we are starting from where we actually are, reading this book. Perhaps it is at home, or sitting on a train, maybe in a bookshop or just filling time waiting for someone. Let us imagine for a moment that we decide to travel in our mind's eye across the planet. We can take any route we like. It doesn't matter if we don't remember the order of the continents or what the seas are called! The important thing is what we experience along the way. If we let the mind wander freely we can picture all sorts of landscapes: town and countryside, deserts and seas, cultivated land and wide open spaces, mountains and valleys.

Above us there is a limitless expanse of sky that binds the planet together in our fragile, life-giving atmosphere. Every molecule of air we breathe has been round the planet many times and been in and out of the lungs not just of many millions of people but billions of animals too, not to mention going through all the plant systems. It's the same with our bodies: our physical make-up comes from particles of animal and plant life that once belonged to other plants or animals and so on backwards through time to the dawn of Creation itself. Light years from now bits of who we are today will form part of an infinite variety of living things. In essence the same material is simply being recycled in different ways over time so that on the most basic physical level *we are one* with our planet.

During our imagined journey, we might encounter millions of our fellow human beings going about their daily business. And if we stopped and felt the touch of their lives upon us, we would see amidst all the diversity of language, custom and religion, certain common bonds. For we all share the same basic needs of survival. And perhaps more than just that: the laughter of a child, the tears of a mother, the tenderness of a lover's touch - these are part of the universal language of humanity. Maybe too we all share the need to reach out and find something beyond the commonplace in our lives: something special and wonderful and magical whatever name we give it.

In the end the sense of oneness lies most deeply in the heart, from that place of inner knowing we call intuition. It is to feel the unity of Creation, which is one of the most indescribable but important milestones in life. To come to a gradual appreciation of the oneness of all things or perhaps to experience it as a moment of revelation is to recognise things as they truly are. For everything is connected, everything is alive.

There is no death. The flow of energy throughout the universe never ceases and life is constantly seeking to express itself in new ways. What we humans call "death" is just the subtle transformation of life from one form into another. The work of the molecules and atoms that make up every organism does not stop when the cells die. Its internal chemistry will continue to operate but in a different way as the body decomposes and is absorbed by bacteria or plants and animals. Its elements form nutrients for new life and so become part of the endless chain of living across the entire universe. And so it is with minerals, rocks, soils and other apparently "lifeless" matter. At a microscopic level we would see continuous exchanges of energy from its constituent particles.

Similarly within different spiritual traditions it is understood that the human soul experiences death simply as a transition to a higher form of life. We may choose to believe in paradise, in reincarnation or anything else but in one sense the concept of "afterlife" is misleading. There is no *after*life. Life is eternal. In calling one side "life" and the other "death", we create an absolute division, where in the deepest sense none exists. They are just different states of being. We are part of a living unity that is constantly transforming itself into an infinite variety of shapes. This is the Oneness. Some people may choose to call it God. We may see it as a force that holds the whole universe together. It doesn't matter what name we give it. It matters only that we are open to experiencing it.

THE WORLD OF DUALISM

Our natural sense of oneness has often been obscured by a worldview that is so commonplace that we can easily absorb it without even noticing. This is dualism, the idea that the universe is divided into two: light and dark, order and chaos, good and evil locked in eternal struggle. Dualism divides humanity too, with one side pitted against the other. For many in the 20th century it took the form of "Communism against Capitalism." Now we are apparently faced with "the clash of civilisations - Islam against the West" or the "War on Terror." The names change but the way of thinking stays the same: two opposing forces, like the story of St. George and the dragon. This is the world of dualism.

In a spiritual sense it means God becomes relegated to being the manager of one side in an unending cosmic football game, with the Devil running the other. Now and again one team seems to score a goal, but there is apparently no decisive outcome, certainly no clear victory for good. God, despite being God, never seems quite able to win the match. Such is the strange conclusion that the logic of dualism would lead us to and one may wonder why so many perfectly intelligent people seem to accept this worldview. In fact it is quite understandable because dualism is a very attractive belief system if you don't think about it too carefully. For it offers a very simple and certain view of the world and it is certainly true that light and dark, good and evil, order and chaos exist. But they do so only at a certain level of human understanding. It is simply one way of looking at things. It is not necessarily how things really are. What we see and experience is from our own very particular perspective. It is not, and perhaps can never be, the whole picture. Dualism ignores a deeper reality, one that goes beyond the world of opposites, that unites all existence: *the oneness of all things*. It is this that offers the opportunity to resolve all conflicts, end all division. Indeed it makes it inevitable. *God is not on one side but by everyone's side.*

9/11: A CHANCE FOR WORLD HEALING

There is a subtle thread that binds the two opposites of good and evil into a process of healing - if we have the mind to use it. For whatever evil we encounter in our lives can always be turned to good through learning to deal with it differently. Indeed one day we may come to see evil as being good in disguise. To see how this works we have only to look at the tragic events of September 11th 2001 when hijacked planes were used to kill thousands of civilians in the U.S.A. For most Americans it was a terrorist outrage, an act of unparalleled barbarity that merited a vigorous military response. President Bush no doubt spoke for the vast majority of Americans when he depicted it as straight fight between good and evil. The United States, home of freedom and democracy, represented the forces of Light. Osama bin Laden and the Al-Qaeda network represented the forces of Darkness.

Equally however, those responsible for the attack no doubt saw America as the Great Satan and felt they were fighting for God's cause. Had not the U.S.A. been responsible, directly or indirectly, for the misery and oppression they saw around them? Had not American influence sought to undermine and destroy the true faith? *They,* Al-Qaeda, were the Light. America was the Darkness. In this way each side mirrored the other's attitudes.

In this they were both to some degree right and both profoundly wrong. The massacre of innocent people in America was an utterly evil act for which there is no possible moral justification in the eyes of Islam or any other world religion. The U.S.A. has indeed been responsible for a great deal of injustice and needless suffering (as well as doing a great deal of good) in its role as a world power.

But in terms of finding a solution the issue is not whether Al-Qaeda is worse than the American government or vice versa. The key point is that they share essentially the same dualistic worldview. And whilst both sides stick to their way of seeing things it will not be possible to bring about a just and lasting peace. Indeed maintaining such an outlook, understandable though it may be, could ensure that this global conflict lasts *forever,* war without end.

Each side will go on blaming the other for the latest atrocity. Each side will go on seeing themselves as the victim, sucking the rest of humanity down with them into the maelstrom of bitter self-righteous retribution. For revenge is a game for which there is no end, no triumphant final conclusion: just an endless piling of carnage upon carnage. If we enter into a cycle of terrorism and counter terrorism there will be no winners. It is as true of this conflict as it is of all others.

What is needed is the courage and the vision to journey away from deeply entrenched attitudes to see the bigger picture. It is in this sense that both sides are equally far from the truth - the truth of the oneness of all things that binds them together and provides the possibility of global healing. 9/11 gives us the opportunity to free ourselves from the mindset of dualism. For dualism cannot provide the answers. It feeds an attitude that puts all the blame for our predicament on others, always wanting to be the victim, never wanting to look at our side of the street, never seeing things from any other viewpoint than our own.

Any fool can justify their own position, at least to themselves, and a lot of fools do. But for a long-term solution to the global challenges we face we need to see things from a wider perspective. This is where the spirit of oneness can help us resolve our problems by approaching them differently - in the way we understand and deal with the issues and the outcome we are working for. Above all we can be open to learning the lessons of terrible events like those of September 11th.

I

The first step is perhaps the hardest:

> *To recognise that we are all human beings.*

That includes the victims *and* the perpetrators of September 11th and every other terrorist attack. And it includes President Bush and Osama bin Laden as well. We are all brothers and sisters. It may feel natural to see the other side as separate from ourselves – a threat, a deadly foe, even as monsters. We may want to exact a terrible retribution from them but in the end this outlook leads us nowhere. Demonising one's opponents may be emotionally satisfying in the short term. But it does not bring the resolution of these life-and-death issues any nearer. We may despise "the enemy" (whoever we think they are), we may be appalled by what they have done. But nevertheless they are part of humanity, part of the universe to which we all belong. Like the old marriage vow, "For better or for worse, for richer or poorer, in sickness and in health" we are all in this together and it is together we will sink or swim.

II

Recognising our common humanity does not mean we roll over and let people walk all over us, much less blow up our buildings and murder our populace. But it does mean that we work towards a world healing in which we can all share, where justice is done for all. For this to happen we will need to become much more open to a deeper global understanding of these issues. This brings us to the second step in world healing:

> *To ask ourselves: "What is the universe trying to tell us?"*

We can listen to what lies behind the voices of hate. We can go behind the mask of the perpetrators of 9/11 and find the roots of this act. For unless we deal with the deeper issues there will always be fertile ground for terrorists to exploit for their own ends. We can seek to understand what fuelled the anger and desire for revenge. For this incident did not occur in a vacuum. It is not enough to see it solely in terms of a handful of fanatics who were either mad or bad. The attackers operated within a historical context, making use of forces that had been building up over many years, perhaps many centuries. The hatred they gave expression to may have its foundation in the centuries-old conflict and mistrust between Christianity and Islam. It also lies in the sense of powerlessness and humiliation that many people feel in parts of the Arab and Moslem world as their once great civilisations have been overtaken and then dominated by the industrialised West. There is a resentment of American power that has come to be blamed for much of the poverty, injustice and oppression that people have suffered. Equally the U.S.A. has, like any other country, felt justified in pursuing its own national interests and supporting its allies across the world. No plan of action that does not address these and all the other complex world issues involved can possibly hope to achieve a lasting solution to the problems illuminated by the events of September 11th. It is essential therefore that we see the causes of this attack as a multifaceted whole and not in simplistic terms of "good guys/bad guys" which is the hallmark of dualism.

III

This brings us to the third step:

To work for a solution in which all humanity wins.

It means we aim for a scenario where the legitimate grievances from each part of the world are addressed. There needs to be an opportunity for people and nations to learn and grow from this tragedy so that the whole of humanity can move forwards towards a better world. The revulsion at a terrorist outrage should not blind us to the fact that there may be great wrongs that need to be remedied. In this the U.S.A. has an important role to play because she is today a great world power, perhaps the greatest the world has ever seen. Yet with that power comes a responsibility. She has the opportunity to use her influence to do so much good in the world. Will she use it wisely? This is the question the President, every member of Congress, above all every American citizen will have to answer. Equally those who preach war against the U.S.A. as a remedy for all their evils need to recognise that many problems would exist with or without America and that some of them they have created for themselves. If we stay stuck in past wrongs we stay stuck forever. *Remedy not revenge is the way forward.* Peace and justice is a process from which we all benefit. If we let go of seeing a resolution in terms of victory for one side or another but rather as a victory for humankind, then we are on the road to success. It is for this reason that it is so important that people not give in to the siren voices of those that would plunge us into war. We can listen to our humanity. It may well be that the present leaders of the two sides will never move from their positions. But we don't need to play their game.

IV

Instead we could work towards an international forum where past misdeeds can be honestly admitted and appropriate reparations made wherever possible. Each nation, particularly those who have been in positions of great international power, could take a "moral inventory" of themselves in their relationships with their neighbours: where they have been selfish, greedy, unfair, bullying; where they have committed atrocities or funded groups that did so, and so on. For we cannot be selective about which terrorists we condemn. If we take the deliberate killing of innocent civilians as a rough definition of what constitutes "terrorism" then most countries, including America, have been guilty either of perpetrating or sponsoring acts of terror at some point. It is for us to take the fourth step:

To clean our side of the street.

It is only in this context that we can fairly demand justice of those who have done us wrong. Osama bin Laden and his Al-Qaeda operatives should be brought to account for their crimes, but equally so should everyone else involved in terrorist outrages and that includes some Americans too. Everybody needs to clean up their act.

Nations would also benefit, as much as many thousands of individuals have already, from such a period of self-examination, coupled with a willingness to repair past wrongs. The Truth and Reconciliation Commission in post-apartheid South Africa has led the way in showing us that there are more positive ways to resolve painful issues than through a welter of mutual recriminations or a never-ending bloodbath. This is no easy task and we cannot expect to reverse the time-dishonoured way of doing things overnight. It will take a while for us to learn to handle our conflicts more constructively, without needing to kill each other in the process. We are going to have to do this in stages: slowly reducing the level of hatred and violence, and gradually coming to more peaceful and holistic solutions where everyone's needs are taken into account.

V

This means we need to pay as much attention to *how* we try to achieve our goals as to what our goals are. The fifth step reveals that:

The means we use will always determine the outcome.

It is all too easy to undermine our high ideals by trying to take moral short cuts. The killing of innocent civilians in one part of the planet is not going to be brought to an end by killing another group of innocent civilians in another. If in our pursuit of justice for ourselves we become brutal and cruel, indiscriminate in our use of force; if we disregard the due process of law and flout human rights then we will end up creating more injustice in the world. The goal of justice for all will be further away than ever. "Might is right" is a dangerous lesson to teach the rest of humanity for sooner or later someone else will use the same principle.

Rather we can base our actions on our common humanity. We need to respect international law so that it applies equally to every individual and nation across the planet without favour. It is better to act as far as possible through global institutions such as the United Nations and the International Criminal Court though ultimately we must be guided by the spirit of oneness not by the letter of any law or the decisions of powerful interests. Even more we need to respect moral and spiritual laws. As Jesus told humankind, do to others as we would have them do to us. This is the principle of oneness in action.

VI

Above all we the people of this planet can take steps to improve the way we communicate with each other. For the attack of September 11th, and incidents like it, was a communication from one part of the earth to another. It was appallingly and indiscriminately destructive. It could hardly have been worse as a form of communication. But nevertheless it was a communication and we have a choice in how to respond to it. Either to close the shutters against the threatening world outside or decide that the way forward is to communicate more, not less - and maybe better than we have done in the past. This is the sixth step:

To create something good from this tragedy.

The revolution in communications offers us unparalleled opportunities to improve our understanding of each other. It could help us break out from our sense of isolation and help us to see things from the point of view of other peoples, other religions, and other cultures. If every person on this planet made an effort to get to know a stranger, an outsider, a foreigner, the whole world would take one small but immeasurably great step forward in ending the divisions amongst humanity.

VII

For 9/11 is a terrible example of how centuries of ignorance and misunderstanding can build a wall of separation between peoples, behind which fear, hatred and thirst for revenge can breed. But we have the chance to break down that wall and come together as one people. This is the sacrifice those thousands of people on September 11th 2001 have made for us, for all humanity. In our seventh and final step we can use this opportunity that has been brought at such great cost:

To create a movement for world unity

For the world of duality is based on the idea of separation, dividing the world into two. By separating ourselves from each other we deny the truth of our own existence: that we are one. If we wrap ourselves up in the flag of our country, our religion, our tribe, whatever group we belong to, and don't see that despite all our differences we belong *to* each other, we disconnect ourselves from our common source. We become isolated clusters of individuals, solitary people who are cut off even from ourselves. Here lies the true darkness into which humanity can fall: when we lose our sense of connection with everything and experience a kind of spiritual death. Hell is separation: this is what the great religions teach us. And whatever our belief system we know from our own lives how important it is to feel part of something. Our destiny is to feel part of everything.

PART II:

THE FIVE PRINCIPLES

OF UNIVERSAL

HUMANITY

THE FIVE PRINCIPLES OF
UNIVERSAL HUMANITY

This is a manifesto for humanity – humanity not only in the sense that it is for all human beings but also in that it appeals to our humanity: our kindness, our compassion and our decency. This sense of humanity has its roots in the oneness of all things. Because we are all connected every act however apparently small will echo across the planet and can contribute to the sum of our global well being. As such it empowers us to create a society based on oneness, giving each one of us a power far greater than that most people would normally conceive of. When we act together we can become an irresistible force for goodness for the world.

This same understanding of oneness brings us to a sense of our responsibility that individually and collectively we all have. It leads us to realise that we will ultimately reap what we sow. If we dump untreated pollutants on this planet recklessly we will make this earth uninhabitable. Our dark deeds will be woven into the fabric of the society in which we live, sometimes at subtle or unseen levels and yet poisoning our lives as surely as any toxic chemical waste.

Thus it is important to use our power wisely. We can begin by learning the lessons of history for the past is littered with grand utopian schemes for improving humanity's lot. Some have proved impractical and ended in failure. Attempts to impose rigid doctrines on to a reluctant populace can pervert the noblest ideals into the worst tyrannies. Nowhere has this been more tragically and graphically illustrated in recent times than in Marxism. Marxism – or communism as it is better known – was the last major attempt to provide a global solution to humanity's problems. It was born out of a sense of outrage at the appalling condition of the poor during the Industrial Revolution of the 19th century. Its founder, Karl Marx, sought to put the redemption of humankind on a scientific basis. A great intellectual edifice was constructed to analyse and remedy the ills of his society. Unfortunately whatever the benevolent intentions of Marx and his successors were, the reality of Communist societies was marked by dogma and repression. That is not to say these brave experiments achieved nothing. There were real material advances for many millions of people across the world. But it fell far short of the original ideals of communism and was achieved at such a hideous cost that it is little wonder that the world has largely recoiled at such doctrines.

BEING "UNPERFECT"

It was from just such a background that Milovan Djilas, a former leading Communist in Yugoslavia, came to reject this dogmatic and utopian approach and gave us a new word: *unperfect*[1]. He recognised the importance of ideas and ideals in order to improve and advance society, but argued that we should not regard them as being wholly realisable. Djilas explained that Utopianism insists society can be perfect and can create a great deal of human suffering in an attempt to attain the impossible. To talk in terms of society being imperfect implies that it can be perfect which in truth it cannot. To use the term unperfect allows us to be what we are as we search for a better future – human.

To take the ideas of Djilas further we could say that there is no point at which we "arrive," except perhaps in the sense that evolution itself comes to an end, if it ever does. The point is to explore and experiment with new ways of understanding and experiencing our sense of connection with each other and the

[1] Milovan Djilas *The Unperfect Society* (Harcourt, Brace & World Inc., New York 1969) translated [from the MS.] by Dorian Cooke.

universe. And to do this we can give ourselves permission to be unperfect, make mistakes and to take responsibility for them.

Thus we can avoid the trap of working out grand elaborate schemes, cajoling, or worse forcing, poor humanity into our idealised picture. Rather our opportunity is to develop as individuals and societies making use of broad principles that illuminate and inform our journey. We can apply our values and beliefs in a variety of ways that take account of the changes in our consciousness and the circumstances of our lives. These could be expressed in any number of ways but the principles set out below offer one possibility:

The Five Principles of Universal Humanity

1. *We recognise humanity as one family and we acknowledge that our loyalty to our humanity transcends all others such as those of nationality, race or religion.*

2. *We accept every part of ourselves as we grow and learn both as individuals and communities, excluding none from the possibility of change and redemption.*

3. *We embrace our oneness with nature with reverence and respect for all life.*

4. *We affirm the fundamental equality, dignity and value of each one of us and seek to end forever the exploitation of one human being by another.*

5. *We respect the liberty of each individual, conscious that as children of one universe our fates are indissolubly bound together.*

It is to these principles that we now turn to explore the avenues they open for us.

THE FIRST PRINCIPLE

We recognise humanity as one family and we acknowledge that our loyalty to our humanity transcends all others such as those of nationality, race or religion.

I am a human being. That I am a human being is more important than whether I am French or Korean, a Buddhist or a Jew, from the Brahmin caste or the working class, a heterosexual man or a lesbian. Our nationality, religion, caste, class, gender or sexuality are all important aspects of ourselves but they are not the whole being. It is our humanity that encompasses all the parts of who we are and is greater than any or all of them. We are human beings before we are anything else. We can be a human being without being a Nigerian or a Christian or a gay man but we cannot be a Nigerian or a Christian or a gay man without being a human being first. This simple fact tells us that what unites us will always be more important than what divides us. Yet if we turn back the pages of history we can see unspeakable crimes committed in the name of nation, race or religion or simply from the fear of what is different. In all these cases we lost sight that our first obligation is towards our common humanity.

In this the lessons of the Holocaust and of the Nuremberg trials that followed are paramount. Those Nazi officials who sought to defend their participation in these terrible crimes by saying, "I was just following orders" found that this defence was not accepted. Whatever orders we are given from the state, from our commanding officer, from our boss, from anyone in authority, there are always higher orders. And these come from our humanity. These instruct us to be compassionate, just, merciful, and fair in our dealings with others; these tell us never to forget the common bonds that we all share. Whatever contract we have signed, whoever's orders we are under, these can never supersede our first responsibility to our humanity.

It was precisely this situation that many German soldiers faced during the Second World War. On the one hand as patriots they felt duty-bound to defend their homeland. They had all taken an oath of loyalty to their head of state, Adolf Hitler. Many no doubt argued that they should fight for Germany on the basis of "my country right or wrong." Yet this philosophy, honourable as it has no doubt seemed to many generations in many parts of the world, had led Germany to the greatest calamity. For Hitler had plunged Europe into a war of aggression, bringing suffering and death to millions that culminated in the horrors of the death camps. There were those that went along with the Nazi regime, even took part in some of the atrocities or maybe simply looked the other way. In doing so they sacrificed that which was decent and honourable in them perhaps out of a narrow sense of duty or fear for themselves and their families. However much we can empathise with their predicament, in the end we must also recognise that they abandoned their wider commitment to their humanity. But they also betrayed their country. For nothing is more sacred to a nation's honour than its sense of right and wrong. If in the process of trying to serve our homeland we break every moral code or ignore our consciences, in the end we are doing no more than fighting for dust and soil for we will have lost that which is truly of value to us.

It is in this light that we can honour the work of the men and women of the German Resistance. Whatever action they took, be it hiding a Jew, defacing a Nazi poster, or taking part in the July Plot to assassinate Hitler, they were all technically guilty of treason. Yet in a deeper sense they stayed loyal to that which was best in the German nation and it was those that obeyed Hitler who were guilty of the highest treason against their country.

The case of Nazi Germany illustrates the dangers of pursuing our loyalty to our country above all else but there are many other examples in the world today. It may be that a company orders its employees to do something that is quite unethical or even illegal. It could be a religious leader who uses dogma to justify an act of barbarity against a fellow human being. Whatever form it takes it will ultimately always resolve itself into one simple question: "Where does my loyalty lie?" To this we, the people of this planet can assert: "Our loyalty is to our humanity".

OUR UNIVERSAL FAMILY

For this is the path that opens before us if we are to live together fruitfully on this earth. We could establish in national and international law that organisations and individuals had an overriding obligation to their humanity. Our Declaration of Human Rights needs a *Declaration of Human Responsibilities* as well to enshrine our obligations to humanity as whole. Something that could be used as a defence in law for refusing to carry out instructions that were damaging to the interests of our planet and its peoples. Governments, commanders of the armed forces, captains of industry, heads of organisations would come to learn that they must behave in a morally responsible way or risk having their orders defied and ending up in the courts.

If we decide that our first loyalty is with our humanity, then we can build a global society that we can be proud of. We need to be clear about what this means: that our commitment to our humanity is more important than our country, our race or our religion, more important than our class or caste, our gender or sexuality or any other aspect of our being. Yet this commitment will bring together the peoples of this planet and give us real hope for the future. This is why we recognise humanity as one family, *our* family, a place where we can deal with our problems peacefully and constructively, secure in the knowledge that we belong to each other, that we are one.

This in turn means expanding our idea of what a family is. Traditionally we have seen the family based on male and female parents, perhaps grandparents too and other relatives, and usually children as well. Today life challenges us to think about families differently. Increasingly they come in all sorts of different shapes and sizes such as those with single, gay or lesbian parents. We have different kinds of families too: people coming together in groups to work through their problems; families of like-minded individuals that share a common goal; families of people working for the highest ideals who may never meet yet on the subtle levels could not be more deeply connected.

In time our consciousness may expand sufficiently to embrace all these different kinds of families, and see them as part of one great human family to which we all belong. Indeed we may come to sense that we belong to an even larger family that encompasses all living things, all life on this planet and beyond. The day will arrive when our concept of family will include those from worlds other than our own. Such "alien" life as exists elsewhere in the universe we will come to recognise as part of the universal family.

A COUNTRY CALLED EARTH

Our sense of oneness, of a common heritage, does not mean that we should neglect our cultures, traditions and beliefs. It is good to honour the tribe – as long as we honour our humanity first. We have the opportunity in the coming generations to let go of the divisions we have created amongst ourselves and come together as one people. We could live in a world free of borders where we respect our differences without building artificial barriers. This is a vision that we can realise in our own time and at our own pace and in a way that empowers us. For it is important that this is a "bottom up" process, a movement of peoples, not a "top down" initiative controlled by business and political elites for their own convenience.

There is nonetheless an overwhelming case for doing so. We need world solutions for world problems. National governments simply do not have the scope or the resources to deal with issues beyond a certain size or complexity. Environmental questions such as climate change cannot be dealt with solely within the borders of one country. This also holds true for the global economy. National economies are to some extent at the mercy of fluctuations in world markets over which they have little or no control. For example, the fall in the price of a single commodity in the trading centres of the West can have a devastating effect on the economies and peoples in non-industrialised countries. Similarly the collapse of confidence in the currency of one country can have serious consequences for other economies as its effects ripple outwards.

The fact that we produce enough food on this planet to feed everybody yet people still are starving to death shows all too clearly the price we pay for a divided world where the short-sighted interests of national governments take precedence over the needs of humanity as a whole. Our interests would be better served if we lived together in one country, *our* country, planet earth: a place where we can look after ourselves as one people; a place where there is an "us" without a "them."

Countries are beginning to discover that by pooling their sovereignty they can have much more influence over major issues than they would on their own. It is a mistake to hang on to the idea of a mythical "independence" when isolated nations are blown hither and thither by the vicissitudes of international events about which they can do little. We have a much greater chance of having a significant impact on the great issues that confront us if we come together as one people. At the same time we can ensure that decisions are taken as locally as possible so that we deal with problems at the level that is appropriate. We do not want some supranational government deciding what colour to paint the village bus but equally the village council cannot deal on its own with a major flooding disaster that covers an entire region. What we need are different levels of government that fit the size of the task to be faced, be it local, regional, national or planetary.

Gradually we can move towards our final goal: a country called earth. Is this possible? Certainly, it is already happening. The Universal Declaration of Human Rights, the growth of international organisations, the global economy, the growing awareness of interdependence, all this points in this direction. But we, the people, can direct this process for the common good. This planet is for all of us and we make the journey together. In turn this means we must be willing to assume our full responsibilities as citizens of the world.

A UNION OF FREE PEOPLES

There are many roads to world unity and humanity will find its own way to it. In my own vision, I see a *union of free peoples*. This is not an imposed union like those of the great empires of yesteryear but a union born of consent, freely given by people who are empowered, democratic, equal. Thus as we enter into this process of union we can respect these guidelines:

1. Those peoples who have not yet gained their national independence must first be given the opportunity to do so. It may be that in some countries where particular groups have suffered many years of oppression and discrimination they will want to break away to form their own independent states and should be free to do so. Later on they could decide to enter into a larger union but as equals.

2. Similarly people living in undemocratic states or where human rights are not upheld, will need to be given the opportunity and support to develop the necessary laws, institutions and culture of rights and responsibilities. Thus they would become truly free to make any decision about their future. Different people are at different stages and we should not insist on a uniform pace for integration into a global union.

3. Neither do we need a "one-size-fits-all" system of government for everyone. We need to assert the fundamental universal human rights that every citizen of this planet can enjoy but beyond that people should be free to make whatever arrangements for local self-government that suit them.

The advantages of coming together as one people are vast. Not only will we be in a position to tackle global issues much more effectively, but also many problems will simply disappear because we will be acting as one country. The huge cost of running different economic systems would go: no customs duties, no trade barriers – all this would make business activity so much easier. A single currency would not only be much more convenient for tourists and trade alike, it would end the parasitic capitalism of currency speculators whose economic activity benefits no one but themselves and who can have extremely destructive consequences for other countries.

A co-ordinated response of global agencies dealing with the basic essentials of life would end forever the obscenity of mass poverty and starvation on this planet. No one need ever go hungry or lack shelter or warmth or the security of employment and a social welfare system. The immense waste of resources, including human life itself, that is now used up in countless wars, large and small, between different states on this planet would end. This is perhaps the greatest dividend of world unity: handling conflicts peacefully and constructively amongst ourselves, as fellow human beings. The hatred and fear whipped up against "foreigners" or "outsiders" would gradually disappear as we came to realise that there were no foreigners, no outsiders, just humans. Governments could no longer hide their misdeeds under the cloak of "the national interest": there would be only one interest, our interest, the interest of the whole planet. So much fear would disappear from our lives, our jobs, our homes as we let go of ancient rivalries and allowed ourselves to be just one universal family.

We would not become less than who we are but more so: no longer having to defend our cultural, religious or ethnic identity from outside attack, we could learn to celebrate and share it without the need to force it on anyone. France would still be France, Mongolia would be Mongolia. We would still have our beliefs and traditions but we would be humans first. In that way we could express our differences within the all-embracing unity of the peoples of this world. What is being asked of us is a fundamental shift in our primary loyalty away from our traditional focus – such as our country or religion – to our humanity. Be a Buddhist, be a Moslem, a Venezuelan, a Cambodian, be whatever and whoever you are, but be a human being first.

THE SECOND PRINCIPLE

We accept every part of ourselves as we grow and learn both as individuals and communities, excluding none from the possibility of change and redemption.

As children we seek to learn and grow in safety and love and so it should be as adults and as societies. We can accept ourselves and be accepted for who we are with all our talents and possibilities. For we are all part of the great diversity of humankind in which we find reflecting back to us a multitude of aspects of ourselves. We also need secure boundaries, a structure in which we can operate with a clear understanding about what is and what is not acceptable. We should not expect that our behaviour is always going to be perfect. As we grow and develop inevitably we will make mistakes. Sometimes we will do things that are just plain wrong. As adults we should be willing to take responsibility for what we do, think and say. But this does not mean we should live in an atmosphere of punishment and fear. We need to acknowledge the hurt or harm we may have done and be willing to make amends. But we also can allow for ourselves and others the possibility of change and redemption. No one is ever beyond hope. We have the opportunity to find a loving and wise response to the challenges we face, both as individuals and as a society, that is in tune with our sense of oneness.

EMBRACING OUR SHADOW
AND OUR LIGHT

The first element of this principle is to *acknowledge everything, deny nothing*. This means that we look squarely at ourselves, at all aspects of our being, without judgement and simply acknowledge "this is me". We come in various colours, shapes and sizes, none of them innately better or worse than any other. We are each differently abled in all sorts of ways and it does not affect our true worth at all. We can be happy, sad, generous, frightened - in all sorts of emotional and mental states at different times, yet they are all part of us.

We may choose to categorise these diverse states and call some "positive" and others "negative". Or we could see one side of our being as "light" and the other as "shadow". One part of ourselves we may find easy to accept and we are willing to show the world. Another part, either because we are ashamed or frightened of it, we try to hide even from ourselves, perhaps in our unconscious. These are the dark cellar doors in our house behind which all sorts of monsters seem to lurk. We may try to keep the doors shut tight, yet somehow something always seems to leak out. We could be filled with guilt or remorse or try to justify to ourselves the traits that disturb us; perhaps we pass it off as a "one-off" or tell ourselves "I must have been drunk" or "they made me like that".

In reality it is all part of our being, and much of the creative energy and power we need is often contained within our shadow side. It's just that we have not yet learnt how to integrate it into the rest of us, how to channel these "dark energies" towards a higher goal, into more constructive avenues. It is this that needs working on, rather than trying to cut ourselves off from the bits that we don't like. For if we don't go beyond the duality of our being and embrace both our shadow and our light we could sever our link with some of the most precious elements in ourselves. Just as it is in the hidden depths of the earth that we find our gems and jewels, so it is that our treasures may lie deep in the dark caverns within us.

Strange as it may sound, it is our self-acceptance that is the beginning of personal change. We can move on more easily when we have embraced the wholeness of our being. We can celebrate the richness and diversity of who we are. We can work with the qualities and challenges we have to make something unique and wonderful of ourselves like a sculptor creating a beautiful piece of art out of clay. To be able to accept that "I am all the colours of my rainbow" can bring a great healing to our lives and end the sense of separation and denial that can exist within us.

This is not to say we should indulge ourselves in every dark thought or passion that we have. It is simply a question of acknowledging what is there. Whether we act on what is inside us is our choice. That is the realm of morality. People with a great light inside them, people of great creative ability or spiritual gifts will often have a correspondingly large shadow side. This does not mean however they are compelled to manifest this aspect of their being. A true spiritual Master, a true artist will have learnt how to sublimate these forces.

Looked at another way it is learning to "ride the dragon". The "dragon" represents those primal energies within us that provide us with the power we need to do our best work. From ancient times, there have been legends about heroes who would try to slay the dragon, as in the story of St. George: that is to say cut themselves off from these forces. At the opposite extreme we can let the dragon be in control, let it dominate our lives. Not for nothing has taking heroin been called "chasing the dragon". But if we can learn to ride the dragon, to integrate it into our being through the work we do on ourselves, we can use its immense strength for the highest ideals, for the most sublime creations.

TAKING RESPONSIBILITY FOR OUR LIVES

The second element is *to take responsibility for the whole of our being.*
It means we acknowledge that what we do, think and feel is
ultimately our responsibility. We stop blaming people or events
for how we react. We recognise we are not robots but that we
have choices. Not everyone responds to the same situation in
the same way. As adults we can decide if a childhood trauma will
ruin our lives or not, or whether the break up of a relationship
means we will never be happy again. Nobody else can make us
resentful or jealous or hurt, only we can. That is not to say
someone else may not have behaved badly. We may need to deal
with what they have done. But we don't need to let whatever
has happened cast a shadow over the rest of our lives.

Taking responsibility for ourselves also means that we let go of
"victim consciousness". Victim consciousness is not the same as
being the victim of a crime such as someone mugged in the
street. Victim consciousness may well have begun with an event
where the individual was indeed a victim of some wrongdoing,
but it becomes a fixed way of seeing oneself in relation to the
world. For such a person life happens to them. They feel
helpless, a permanent victim of events that are out of their
control. Of course there are things that happen in life that are
out of our control but what is most definitely not is the way we
react to them. In this we have ultimate freedom and complete
power within ourselves. No one can enslave our minds, our
spirits, our will except us. We are always free to make some kind
of choice whatever the limitations of the external circumstances.

The trouble is, feeling like a victim can be very appealing. It has
a sense of moral righteousness about it, the comfort of believing
we are always the injured party. It can become almost addictive,
a way of going through life without ever really taking

responsibility for it. So naturally it can be difficult to let go of, particularly if we have had events in our lives where something terrible really did happen to us. The thing to bear in mind though is that victim consciousness is a false perspective on life and on oneself. And it is not the whole truth. For often people who think of themselves as victims fail to notice that they themselves can act abusively in some other part of their lives.

This can be seen both with individuals and with communities, even governments. At some point in the past somebody or some group has persecuted another. They in turn retaliate. Perhaps they do so in kind, or commit an even worse atrocity. They justify it to themselves by telling themselves they were the victims of an unprovoked attack (which they may well have been) and were only punishing the offender. Their behaviour of course enables the other group now to see themselves as the victims, so they retaliate in turn. This usually leads to further counter-measures from the other side and soon we are locked in a cycle where everyone thinks they are the victim and no one can ever quite see themselves as being an aggressor.

Alternatively the victim simply takes out their aggression on someone else weaker than them, so everyone ends up dumping on everyone else and no one takes responsibility for their behaviour. This can be seen at work, in families, between different ethnic or religious groups – the list, sad to say, is almost endless. The key to breaking out of this cycle of victim-aggressor in the first place is to see the destructive dynamics for what they are. Second, to seek alternative routes to a solution where the hurt and harm felt by both sides is recognised, and where the goal is a fair and equitable settlement for all. And third, to keep one's own side of the street clean, making amends if appropriate regardless of what others have done.

NOTHING IS BEYOND FORGIVENESS

Humanity's salvation lies in choosing a path which is neither that of the victim nor that of the aggressor but which takes full responsibility for its own growth and development and that includes its own shortcomings too. This is crucial if we are to accept every part of our being. If we can learn to deal with our mistakes and wrongdoing constructively we can integrate them into a process of growth where every experience can be ultimately used for the good. We have all done things we regret in our lives, we would hardly be human if we did not, but that does not mean we have to write ourselves off because we have done something wrong. However terrible an event may seem to us, there is nothing that is beyond forgiveness, nothing that cannot be healed, nothing that cannot be transformed into something of value for ourselves and others.

Whether we use such occasions in this way is a different matter. The victims of crime can allow themselves to be eaten up with bitterness. The perpetrators can crucify themselves with guilt or be indifferent to the sufferings of others. None of these attitudes does anyone any good. If we work through our rage, our self-hate, whatever emotions may be thrown up by such an incident we can move on and come to a recognition that:

The possibility of change and redemption is open to everyone.

This is the third element in our healing and it is the cornerstone of our personal growth. For it provides us with that essential ingredient: hope. It means we should never give up on ourselves however low we feel we may have sunk, whatever we may have done, however bad things may seem. It is *never* too late to turn back from the path of self-destruction, never too late to change. It is always possible for some good to come out of our lives.

What is true for us as individuals is true for society as a whole. We should never abandon hope with others just as we should never abandon hope with ourselves. The possibility of change and redemption applies to everybody without exception. Individually or collectively we may need to be held to account and make amends. But we also can offer ourselves and others the chance to change and redeem something of our lives. Whether that opportunity is taken is a different matter. As a society, our responsibility is simply to create opportunities for people to make good any damage they may have caused and give them the possibility to rebuild their lives.

This is important to bear in mind when we encounter the most terrible crimes such as child abuse, rape and murder. Understandably many people react with shock or anger and demand that those who commit such crimes be locked away forever or even executed. It is indeed right and proper that we recoil from these acts with horror. Yet the people who have done these things are in truth our brothers and sisters, part of us, our society, part of the Oneness. If we demonise them or deny them the chance of redemption, we do this to some part of ourselves. We may feel like putting these people in jail and throwing the key away but if we do this we imprison some part of our own being forever. If we execute someone some part of us dies too, extinguishing the precious candle of hope within ourselves.

Similarly it can be very tempting to accept the image we often are presented with of a "decent, law-abiding majority" in contrast to a "tiny minority of troublemakers" as being the whole truth. This apparently reassuring picture of "us" and "them" is however based on a myth: that somehow we are separate; that there are two species of humanity, and perhaps we see one of them sub-human. But in reality we are all part of one organic entity that makes up society and that at a subtle level we express something of each other.

Even the extreme behaviour of an individual or small group will always feed off an aspect of society as a whole. A racist, sexist or homophobic attack may be the work of one person, and they undoubtedly must take responsibility for their actions. But what we as a society do or say will create an atmosphere in which these acts can take place. If our attitudes are bigoted - even if we do not act out on them ourselves - we still contribute to the sum total of hate or prejudice in society. And if a person less controlled in their behaviour than us takes it out on someone we too must take our share of the responsibility for encouraging these forces.

Nevertheless the perpetrator must take responsibility for his or her own crimes. Recognising society's role in creating the conditions in which people may act in a destructive way is not the same as saying society is to blame. We all have our individual area of responsibility, our part of the Oneness to contribute. Consciously or unconsciously we make our choices and nothing can take away the responsibility that goes with that freedom. Yet in dealing with these situations of wrongdoing we can avoid falling into the trap of perpetuating the cycle of victim-aggressor in relation both to our own misdemeanours and to the crimes in society at large.

JUSTICE WITHOUT PUNISHMENT

Most importantly we can let go of the desire to punish, which is at the heart of popular attitudes to our criminal justice system. In reality it is no more than the desire for retribution or revenge. Whilst it is only natural we should feel these emotions it is not true justice and it heals nothing. We do have entirely legitimate concerns and interests in dealing with criminal behaviour but satisfying one's personal thirst for vengeance is not one of them. More constructively, we could meet three important and entirely justifiable goals as a society: to live in safety and security, free from the threat of violence and intimidation; to challenge anti-social behaviour; and to achieve just recompense for any wrongdoing we have suffered. There are many ways of approaching this and what is set out below is only one of a number of possibilities.

The principles of containment, change and compensation

The principle of containment is simply to ensure that anyone that has been convicted of a crime that poses a real threat to others – a violent assault for example – is taken off the streets and held securely and humanely until such time as they are assessed as no longer being a danger to the public. The onus would be on them to demonstrate that they had learnt the appropriate lessons and were willing to use different, more constructive ways of dealing with their problems. At the same time the state must be willing to put in the necessary resources to provide a programme of alternative strategies or additional skills to help provide people with a second chance in life. For example in the case of someone who habitually used to resort to violence in facing difficult situations, they could be offered anger management courses. It might be a case of laying on adult literacy lessons or appropriate counselling. We can at least provide the opportunity for people to examine their lives and make the necessary changes. Attendance at the appropriate retraining courses would be an essential precondition to any future release. The emphasis on punishment can mean that criminals can get out after they have served their time regardless of whether they have shown the slightest inclination to reform or not.

As in all walks of life you cannot force people to change. No matter how many times a drug addict is sent to a rehabilitation centre, unless they are willing to make the necessary changes in their life they are likely to return to their old drug using ways once they are let out. We have to be realistic and recognise that some people will need to go through a great deal of re-education before they learn their lessons. Some may never do so. But it does not mean we should not insist that they at least experience positive alternatives to anti-social behaviour. And above all we should never give up hope that change is always possible. Equally it is important that people should not be let out of custody if it is felt that they still represent a significant danger to others. In this way there would be a considerable incentive for them to make a serious effort to mend their ways.

Those whose crimes are no real threat to the general populace – non-payment of a parking fine, for instance - should not be locked up. It is a disproportionate response as well as being a waste of resources to incarcerate people for minor offences. But it does not mean that this group too should not be required to undergo re-education courses if necessary. Repeatedly dropping litter for example may indicate a need for developing some greater environmental awareness and consideration for others.

Both for minor and more serious crimes the focus needs also to be on compensation. Today everyone is so busy demanding punishment, surprisingly little attention is given to ensure the victim secures just recompense. Perpetrators of crimes need to compensate the injured party. Ideally they should pay in full whatever amount the courts decide is fair and be set to work to do so. Obviously if someone has caused millions of pounds worth of damage which they could not possibly pay off in one lifetime then a sum that is proportional to the person's capabilities has to be set. Equally someone should not be able to take advantage of their personal wealth to simply buy their way out of making proper amends. The work done to compensate victims should be set aside from their ordinary employment and determined by the courts.

Beyond the immediate demands of justice there lies another possibility open to us - healing. For this to happen for the criminal he or she needs to acknowledge their responsibility for what they have done and become willing to repent. For the injured party they can let go of the trauma of the past. Both sides can forgive. Society as a whole needs to let go of its knee-jerk reaction to dump all its anger and hatred on the criminal. There is a difference, as a religious tradition has long held, between the sin and the sinner. It is one thing to pass judgement on an individual's actions. It is another thing to pass judgement on the individuals themselves. We cannot possibly know what life experiences people have been through. What may seem natural and normal to us may not be for someone else and vice versa. We should not automatically expect everyone is going to share the same standards and values as we do. That is why it is so important both in our personal and public lives to make our expectations explicit and clear. The way we deal with the shadow side of society, like the way we deal with the shadow side of ourselves, is the key to learning to grow into one organic whole both as individuals and as communities.

THE THIRD PRINCIPLE

We embrace our oneness with nature with reverence and respect for all life.

We can expand our sense of unity with our being and humanity as a whole to encompass a wider unity that is nature. Looking beyond the confines of our planet we can go further and embrace the unity of the universe with all its different elements and beings.

The first step is to recognise that we form an integral part of the network of plants, animals and minerals that covers the entire planet. We may choose to see ourselves as different and it is certainly true we are unique. But that does not make us separate and in the long term we rely on the rest of nature for our survival as much as any plant or animal. The food we eat, the air we breathe, the land we use is all part of a complex web of interdependence that is part of our life on this earth.

However humanity has increasingly seen itself as somehow apart from nature. This idea, which has taken root particularly in the industrialised world, has been very damaging both for the planet and ourselves. The immense physical destruction of large parts of the earth are starting to rebound on us not simply on the material level with problems such as pollution and climate change but also on the more subtle levels: the impoverishment of the natural environment has its echo in the spiritual impoverishment people are increasingly beginning to feel as we lose our connection with the rhythm of the seasons and the sense of belonging to the whole. Recent research has indicated that much of our modern stress and many psychological problems respond positively to contact with nature, even if it is just a picture in our room or passing through the countryside on the way to work. All this tells us how important it is to keep our sense of being in contact with the natural world.

RESPECT AND REVERENCE
FOR ALL LIFE

It is from this sense of oneness with nature that our reverence and respect for all life springs. In part we are simply acknowledging our common ancestry with all of Creation. Yet we can recognise our oneness with nature without compromising our instinct for survival or expecting other animals or plants to do so. We should not blame a fox for eating the farm chickens nor should we feel guilty if we use plants or animals to live. We are part of the great chain of life that is entwined in the very fabric of the universe. That also makes us part of the never-ending pattern of creation and destruction through which the underlying unity of life assumes its different shapes and forms. Whatever we do will in one sense create a life and bring a death. If we make a wooden table we destroy a tree in the process. It is true of all aspects of our existence.

But we have a choice whether to play our role with consciousness and respect or whether arrogantly and unthinkingly to trample all underfoot. To kill an animal or destroy a plant so that we may eat or clothe ourselves or build shelter is one thing. To use animals for sport or entertainment, to treat them callously or to destroy plant life needlessly and without regard for the consequences is another. Our awareness and sensitivity may lead us to be vegetarian or fruitarian or to insist that the animals we eat be treated humanely. We may focus on the need for sustainable development or the advantages of organic farming. It may take many forms. The key point is that our approach is one of reverence and respect for all living things.

By contrast the dualistic approach to nature has often been expressed in terms of conflict and aggression between two separate entities – "Man against Nature" or "the rape of Mother Earth". Notice too the role gender plays: nature, the "victim", is depicted as female; humanity, the "aggressor", as male. But just as men have traditionally underestimated the power of women, so too have people come to believe nature is something that can be controlled and abused at will. But nature is far from passive and our so-called "domination" may prove to be a very fragile thing indeed. In the end it may be us that are eliminated as a species if we do not learn to live in harmony with the rest of this planet and nature will continue in its different forms and shapes as it did before we arrived on the scene.

If it is an illusion to see ourselves as separate from nature it is arrogant folly to think we are morally superior to it. We may be special but that does not make us better and it does not give us a licence to kill or exploit or wreak havoc across the length and breadth of the planet. What we do have is power and choice and with that comes responsibility. No species can destroy like human beings can. Yet none have quite our creative ability either. Our impact on this planet, for good or for ill, is immense. We could do great damage to this earth before we are ourselves destroyed and leave behind a barren landscape as our legacy for centuries to come. Or we could create a world of great beauty and harmony that is a marvel to behold.

For the possibility of change and redemption is open to us in our relationship with nature as it is with ourselves. It would have been far better if humanity had taken a more constructive attitude earlier on in its history but it does not mean we have to throw up our hands in despair and wallow in doom and gloom. The nature of nature is change and no matter how we had behaved the world we live in now would be very different from the way it was a hundred or a thousand or a million years ago.

Much of what we have done is destructive and irresponsible but the earth has managed some spectacular events of its own, wiping out great swathes of plant and animal life at various stages of its evolution without a human in sight. The point is to play our role in the process of change with consciousness and sensitivity. But we need not fall into the trap of confusing conservation with conservatism and adopting a sentimentalised picture-postcard view of nature. We cannot preserve everything exactly as it is or was. But we can do our best to preserve the richness and bio-diversity of the planet so that we can help to keep all nature's options open.

We can also take responsibility for the way we behave in our own personal lives. At the most basic level it may consist of not dropping litter in the street or using recyclable materials where we can. We can take it further and become aware of pollution on the subtle levels, in our thoughts and feelings. Dumping our anger all over someone else or conversely creating harmony in our lives is as potent in its long-term consequences as reducing the amount of lead in car emissions or developing organic farming. We can learn to take responsibility for our own garbage at all levels. Equally it is hypocritical for industrialised countries to preach environmental awareness to countries whose populations are struggling for their very existence without first looking at what they could be doing at home to improve the situation. We always need to look at our side of the street first and see what we are responsible for. Our growing awareness of environmental issues, the spread of green movements are all encouraging signs of a heightened consciousness. To succeed, however, it needs to become part of a wider understanding of oneness that applies to every area of life.

Looking beyond our planet with its fragile ecosystem there lies the vast expanse of our universe. It would be criminal folly to maintain the same exploitative attitude that has characterised our relationship with planet earth elsewhere in the cosmos. And we will surely not be on our own forever. No doubt the day will come when humanity makes contact with life on other planets. It would change everything and yet nothing. We will be exposed to different expressions of life and yet we will be able to see the common bonds that unite all the beings of the universe. The issues for life across the cosmos will always be essentially the same. This is one universe. We will be called upon to open our minds in a way we never have before and yet we can always be guided by our principles of universal humanity.

THE FOURTH PRINCIPLE

We affirm the fundamental equality, dignity and value of each one of us and seek to end forever the exploitation of one human being by another.

"We hold these truths to be self-evident: that all men are created equal; that they are endowed by their Creator with certain inalienable rights, that among them are life, liberty and the pursuit of happiness."

American Declaration of Independence, 1776

The words of the American Revolution rang out across the world as a clarion call to free people everywhere and they have echoed down the ages. Today we have the opportunity to fulfil their promise. However unperfectly the ideals of equality and liberty were articulated by the authors of the Declaration and however unperfectly they have been realised in the years since they were written, they express a Divine ideal, a universal truth that lies at the heart of the universe. For the seeds of liberty and equality are to be found in Creation itself. All matter is made up of atoms but arranged in different combinations. That it is made up of the same thing gives us our equality. That it is in different combinations gives us our liberty. Put another way, we could say our equality springs from the fact we are all part of the Oneness. Our liberty comes from the freedom each one of us has to give our own unique flavour to it. Evolution uses the same basic building blocks of life to explore and experiment with a myriad of different forms, of which we are one. Thus liberty is an evolutionary necessity. Equality is an evolutionary fact. Today we humans can make conscious choices that mould our destiny taking this freedom to new heights. From a spiritual viewpoint this is the freedom God has given us. *It is the freedom to be our own creators.*

Our recognition of the importance of liberty and equality is held within our sense of oneness. From this flows the basis of the way we connect with each other. Thus we affirm the fundamental equality, dignity and value of each one of us. That means ending forever the exploitation and oppression of our fellow humans. Our challenge is to translate this idea into reality.

Exploitation and oppression have their basis in separation, the separation of one human being from another. Disconnected from our common humanity we can feel free to take advantage of others, to treat them as if they were inferiors without dignity or respect. Behind our wall of separation we do not see our fellow human beings as they really are. It is as if they become objects, pawns in a game, not real people with needs and feelings. The process of exploitation and oppression can take different forms. It can be the denial of individual human rights or national self-determination; it can be the abuse of power from someone in authority; it can be the economic exploitation of working people. But in each case it involves treating people as less than fully human. It is a denial of oneness.

FREEDOM FROM OPPRESSION

Oppression, like exploitation, is based on division and the abuse of power. It can be the minority that oppresses the majority or the majority that oppresses the minority. The division may run along the lines of class or caste, ethnicity or religion, gender or sexuality – there is unfortunately no end of ways humanity can divide itself. But it is always based on a lie. The lie says that we that these are not fellow human beings, that the world is divided into an "us" and "them". It is one of the worst lies humanity has ever told itself. It has caused untold misery and destruction. The last century brought us the horror of the Holocaust and the

Killing Fields of Cambodia. There are many examples, large and small, that continue today.

It almost always involves dehumanising those whom we despise – as vermin, as carriers of disease for example; or as part of some abstract phenomena. "Fighting Communism", for instance, sounds so much better than the reality of killing our fellow humans, Communist or otherwise. We "eradicate homosexuality", disguising the misery and suffering we are inflicting on real people. We can all too easily project our own demons outwards onto some other group and make them our scapegoats. We think if we could only get rid of them all our problems would be solved. But whatever issues we have will only ever be solved on the basis of recognising each other as brothers and sisters.

THE PROFIT MOTIVE

Exploitation presents us with other challenges. In large parts of the world the worst excesses of human exploitation, like slavery, have been abolished though even this practice still hangs on. But much work remains to be done. Even in the relatively prosperous industrialised world, the exploitation of people has simply found new, subtler expressions. No longer are there the appalling conditions of the slums and factories of the Industrial Revolution – though these continue to prevail in many counties that are in the process of industrialising – but instead we are faced with the insecurities of short-term contracts and company relocation together with an ever-increasing workload. For example the workers in the West are told if they do not work harder and produce more they will lose out to workers on the Pacific Rim. And needless to say the workers of Asia are told the same! What we are left with is a demoralised, stressed population whose lives are being sucked into workaholic frenzy – yet millions are still unemployed.

At the heart of exploitation lies the profit motive. The logic of the profit motive will always push companies towards seeking ways of using the least number of people to do the most amount of work – regardless of the cost to the individuals concerned or society at large. When profit becomes the ends it becomes a force for exploitation and creates many of the problems we encounter in the workplace today. Of course businesses need to balance their books in order to meet their costs and make a living. But that is not the same as making the pursuit of ever-increasing profits the primary purpose of the organisation. The consequence of adopting this goal can lead people to believe that *any* activity that boosts profits is good. Dumping shoddy goods in world markets for example would be quite acceptable; so is polluting the environment within (and sometimes outside) the law; charging extortionate prices or paying their workers a pittance would make sound economic sense if you could get away with it.

This philosophy of the profit motive encourages greed, irresponsibility and callousness. It could not be otherwise because the whole ethos of the organisation is built upon the pursuit of material wealth above anything else. It is a purely amoral objective with no connection to the needs of the planet or its people. Whilst this situation is allowed to continue, corners will continue to be cut in the way the customer, the employee or the environment is dealt with. As a result the workforce feels constantly under pressure and few feel secure, valued or properly rewarded. The whole system is driven by fear and greed, pitting not only worker against manager, but also worker against worker, manager against manager. And in the end *no one* really profits from this process, not even those ostensibly making the money. For even those at the top have their own insecurities and anxieties knowing that their position is dependent on never-ending success and that they are surrounded by other "predators" all too willing to take their place. Inevitably employees are asked to make ethical compromises just to get on and keep their jobs. Unbridled capitalism makes moral prostitutes of us all. Too often we give away that which is most precious, most valuable, most wonderfully unique in us to make ends meet, to keep up appearances, to get on with the boss. The system can corrupt us and we can feel helpless and disempowered as we watch ourselves be consumed by it.

This system of exploitation makes use of the power one person has over another. Perhaps it involves exploiting someone's vulnerability or their need for a job or approval. In fact any employer-employee relationship, however outwardly benign, is based on a difference in power and is therefore exploitative. The fact that one person is calling the shots inevitably defines the relationship. Employers and employees can be friendly towards each other but they can never be true friends, for there is an absence of basic equality, which is the basis of real comradeship. This is not to say every business is out to grind the faces of its workforce into the dirt or is irresponsible or immoral. Some individuals and companies have made determined efforts to treat their workers more fairly and behave more ethically both towards the customer and the environment. But it is despite rather than because of the current economic system. For the sole pursuit of profit will exert such a force on the organisation that people trying to follow an ethical agenda are always swimming against the prevailing current. To remedy the evils of profit-driven capitalism a more fundamental change is required.

THE BUSINESS OF ONENESS

Fortunately there is a remedy and it lies in putting the principle of oneness first in the way we do business. There are many approaches to this and what follows is only one of a number of possibilities.

Aims of the business

Why we do something is the basis of our moral choices and ultimately determines the outcome. We have seen where the single-minded pursuit of profit can take us. But we could choose instead to pursue other ends. First we can free ourselves from the slavery of the profit motive: not-for-profit companies have shown one way in which businesses can function without profit as the primary purpose. It liberates us to pursue a goal where *everybody wins*. We can commit ourselves to excellence in the quality of our particular products or services. A wider commitment to the environment, the community and the workforce can be enshrined in the company's aims and objectives. This in turn requires a transformation in the role of the investor or shareholder. We already have a growing market of people and organisations that want to put their money into ethical businesses and it is this kind of approach that holds out hope for the future.

Work relationships

We can also change the nature of our work relationships. We have seen that the traditional employer-employee model is innately exploitative but we can find other ways of working together. In the past whenever new approaches have been tried, like in the Soviet Union or Communist China, the exploitation of the workforce has simply continued in new ways. For the state can be quite as exploitative as the private capitalist. But we could base our work relationships on liberty and equality. We can see this in co-operatives where free associations of individuals come together to work for their mutual benefit. Various forms of profit sharing and worker participation in decision-making are also a step in the right direction. Workers or their representatives should be allowed to negotiate contracts freely rather than being faced with a fait accompli by their employer as is so often the case. We can stop working *for* other people but instead work *with* other people. Instead we can work *for* a high ideal, such as the good of humanity or the wellbeing of the planet, building our vision of heaven on earth.

Business in the wider world

Finally we need also to consider the position of businesses in relation to society as a whole. Many large multinationals are as rich and powerful as governments but they are not elected or directly accountable to the public at large. They can wield enormous and not always benign power across the world markets and have a profound influence on society. In pursuit of ever greater profits thousands of hard-working women and men can be made redundant at the stroke of a pen with devastating results for not only those directly employed but also all the businesses and individuals dependent on them. Taxpayers can find themselves picking up the tab for the cost of unemployment whilst the company moves on to make more money in some other corner of the globe. At present large companies exercise power without responsibility. Yet the interests of the planet as a whole can take precedence over the narrow commercial interests of the multinationals in a number of different ways:

- Governments could encourage and support the formation of not-for-profit companies to free businesses to pursue more holistic goals.
- Co-operatives and companies with proper worker representation on their boards can become more responsible to those that create their wealth.
- *The Declaration of Human Responsibilities* would help businesses to understand the importance of acting in accordance with the needs of the whole earth and all of humanity.
- There is an important role for the consumer in this by supporting best practice in businesses.

Whatever paths we choose, we have the power to reclaim business for humanity.

THE FIFTH PRINCIPLE

We respect the liberty of each individual, conscious that as children of one universe our fates are indissolubly bound together.

If equality is at the root of our relationship with our fellow humans, liberty is at the core of humanity's journey. The freedom to explore, to evolve, is at the heart of the unfolding of Creation. Unless we have that liberty the human spirit cannot express itself freely and fully. Yet this precious freedom also brings a responsibility for the journey we take through life will inevitably impact on the rest of the world. These two sides of life are reflected in the human psyche: the need to be uniquely ourselves and the need to belong. Yet they can be brought together both in our individual lives and as a society. Because we are all connected, as we develop as individuals, as we become our true selves, we inevitably contribute more to the whole. If the ingredients we are putting into the pie are getting better and better, everyone benefits. Thus within the Oneness our highest good will always be to the highest good of all. Looked at scientifically, we can see that the different elements that make up the single organism of the universe will ultimately work together however things may appear to us at any given moment. During the course of evolution, everything and everybody finds its right place and function.

LAWS OF ONENESS

Humanity's challenge is to find ways of supporting this process: both giving people the freedom to develop into their own unique being and maintaining that essential awareness of the Oneness that binds us together. Nowhere is this more vividly illustrated than in the framing of our laws.

The existence of a law is an admission of human failure. If we were all truly aware of our connection with each other and our planet, if we could clearly see the consequences of our thoughts, feelings and actions, we would always act in accord with our sense of oneness. For everything from murder to dropping litter in the street is a denial of oneness. The ultimate crime is the belief in the illusion of separation. One day, as we grow in understanding, written laws will disappear from humankind. But for now we must deal with each other as we are. For now laws can be used to protect people and the planet, enforcing values from the outside that actually we carry on the inside.

One way of approaching law-making is to follow the classic liberal formula of letting people do what they want as far as possible unless their behaviour harms others. It allows people to explore and experiment with their own lives yet at the same time maintaining our overall sense of responsibility towards each other. This involves setting minimum standards of behaviour rather than imposing laws to get people to act in the "right" way. It is the difference, for example, between ensuring that someone's smoking doesn't damage other people's health and stopping people smoking altogether. By contrast the authoritarian view, much beloved of political and religious fundamentalists, is that the law should reflect their particular interpretation of God's Will or conform to a narrow political ideology. For them there is a single path that we must all follow. They claim there is an absolute and objective truth - to which they alone have access - that should decide how we live our lives.

THE TOLERANCE OF UNCERTAINTY

This brings us to a wider question about liberty and truth. Is there an absolute truth that we must all base our lives upon? Who gets to decide what Divine Will or the immutable laws of history are? What if someone's beliefs are different to ours? For fundamentalists, the road to the truth is a straightforward one. All the answers are to be found in a single book like the Christian Bible or the Qu'ran or the Thoughts of Chairman Mao. There is an attractive simplicity and certainty to this way of seeing things and often its proponents show great energy and courage in pursuit of their beliefs. Yet such people are rarely respecters of liberty. And indeed why should they be if they are convinced that there is only one path through life and anyone who deviates from it must be in error? Yet if we think about this view we can see that it is fundamentally flawed.

First, even if we accept absolute truth exists, our consciousness may be too limited to grasp it fully. Why do we suppose that the human brain is capable of understanding everything in the universe? There may be things that are too subtle, too deep for us. There is a great deal about life we may *never* know. Indeed accepting life's mysteries is perhaps part of our growth into true wisdom. "I don't know" may be the most intelligent thing a human being can say. It does not prevent us from trying to find out whatever we can or coming forward with our own theories. It just means that we don't have to know everything; and we don't have to be dogmatically certain about everything. Each generation will ask different questions and may explore further but there may always be something that is tantalisingly just beyond our reach. A moment of true revelation may be to see a profound truth and at the same time realise it is an infinitesimally small part of the whole. In this way we could say we gradually grow towards the ultimate truth, or if we prefer, that we grow towards God. It could be, as Milovan Djilas says, in our unperfect world we will strive without ever reaching this. Or we will realise there is no goal that we reach in terms of absolute truth but a never-ending journey of exploration and self-discovery.

Secondly, even if we suppose that there are some fundamental truths that are important for humanity to follow, it would be arrogant to claim that we know beyond question what they are. We cannot hide behind a religious text like the Bible or the Qu'ran claiming it is the Word of God and therefore everyone must automatically obey it; or that a secular text like Marx's Das Kapital reveals the immutable laws of history that we must all follow. For in each case it is our *choice* to believe these doctrines. And if these books are indeed Divinely inspired or contain some great wisdom, it is again our choice how we understand them. Saying something is literally true is as much our own interpretation as trying to make sense of a text within its historical context or seeking an inner symbolic meaning. Whatever beliefs we have are ours and ours alone. They are our personal choices for which we are individually accountable. No one can legitimately claim to have access to the ultimate truth. We cannot abdicate our moral and spiritual responsibilities by saying we are obeying orders even if we think they come from the highest source, be it God or theories of the class struggle.

We may feel that a sacred text, be it the Bible or the Communist Manifesto, contains all the answers and we should follow its precepts to the last dot and comma. But if we give our power away to words on a page we lose touch with our own humanity. And we know from history that those who have asserted a dogmatic certainty in their beliefs have often left a trail of destruction in their wake. Whether this is in the name of political ideologies like Marxism or religious doctrines makes little difference in practice. In medieval times the crusaders slaughtered their way to salvation across the Middle East crying "God wills it" as their opponents declared *jihad* against them. No doubt the more sincere on both sides genuinely believed they were obeying God's calling in doing their bloody work. Similarly millions of lives were sacrificed in the pursuit of the Communist ideal by people who for the most part probably believed in what they were doing. But it is one thing to believe passionately in one's cause. It is another to suppose that one's beliefs are the absolute truth that can be imposed on everyone else.

Thirdly, if we believe the truth is to be found within a rigid doctrine paradoxically we prevent it from actually unfolding in our lives. For we no longer experience life as it is but see it through a veil of dogma. Facts, events, people have to fit into our preconceptions. It's rather like taking a photograph and insisting that it represents total reality for all time. At best what we see is only part of the whole and it ignores the inevitable changes in the scene that it depicts. Such fixed attitudes actually cut us off from the truth, from life, from our experience of the Oneness. Similarly following the "correct" doctrine is no guarantee of actually doing any good in the world. Believing in the Virgin Birth does not of itself make us better people. Many of those who do a great deal of good in the world have no formal faith, nor do they need it. These are "light workers" who have a natural sense of goodness that comes from within. Far too much importance can be attached to whether people believe the "right" things, far too little on what people actually do or why they do it. The key to building heaven on earth is not to be found through doctrinal correctness but through how each of us lives our daily lives.

It is therefore surely better for us to live with the tolerance of uncertainty, allowing for the fact that we do not always know what path people have to follow. What we can do is share with others what we have learnt from our own lives and leave them to take what they want from it. And the truths that come from personal experience have an innate authority that dogma does not have. Fervently reciting political or religious articles of faith that have been handed down to us is no substitute for a truth that has been actually lived. And if we really know something for ourselves, it seems to make us less disposed to try and force our views on humanity. The desire to impose our beliefs on everyone else seems conversely to stem from an inner uncertainty, as if by convincing others we can convince ourselves; or by stifling dissent without we can stifle dissent within. In truth what we may be able to say is that we have found an approach to life that is right for us. What we cannot say that it is right for anyone else.

WINDOWS ON HUMANITY

By the same token we need to be careful about making judgements about people's lives when we have only a partial view of the whole. When we encounter people we are seeing only a snapshot of where they are right now. What we do not know is where they have come from and how far they have travelled in their lives. Someone may come across as rather prickly and understandably we are put off. Yet if we looked back we might discover that they have made huge strides in their lives transforming what was once the extreme and violent behaviour of their background into something that, whilst not being very sociable, is certainly an enormous improvement. It does not make their current behaviour more acceptable but maybe it makes them more understandable. Equally we do not know the direction of people's lives. Someone may appear to have everything going for them – good looks, success, wealth – but if their lives are controlled by greed or fear eventually it may end in miserable emptiness, having learnt little or nothing, their talents wasted.

Similarly if we base our morality purely on people's outward behaviour we may miss the value of an act that can only be understood by looking at its inner nature. By asking questions such as, "Where is the love in this?", "Where is the wisdom?", "Where is the honesty?", we can gain a better sense of the true morality of the act. Morality is to be found as much in why we do something as what we do. We can see this in the way people understand the morality of sexual relationships. Those whose morality is based on a dogmatic model will tend to look at the outer form and will favour one kind of relationship over another - for example the married couple over two people simply living together or the heterosexual relationship over the lesbian or gay relationship. On the other hand if our morality is based on our inner life we may ask, "Is this a loving relationship? Is it stable, happy, respectful?". Whether it happens to be between an opposite or a same-sex couple or what the exact nature of the formal contract between them is not then the issue.

FINDING OUR OWN PATH

The point of our freedom is to develop our potential and become who we truly are. It is only in this way that we can fully contribute to the world as a whole. Of course it is only natural that we should look to others for guidance as we begin our journey of exploration but in time we must be prepared to stand on our own two feet. We can still listen, read, reflect on the wisdom of the great teachers but we acknowledge that ultimately the choices are our own. We must find the answers for ourselves. If great saints or philosophers have trodden the path before us, it is to show us it can be done, not that we should attempt to become pale imitations of them. We take full responsibility for our moral and spiritual development.

Quite what form our path will take will vary from person to person and here we have to consider the limits of our freedom of action. There are those placed by nature - the limitations of our physical bodies, the materials at our disposal, the pace of change. However our minds, our imagination, are always as free we allow them to be. Overall our freedom of choice will always exist within certain parameters - those set by ourselves, perhaps influenced by our culture, the prevailing consciousness of our times, our parenting and so on. But these parameters are not fixed. The more innovative and daring our decisions are, the wider our horizons become. Equally someone who is overcautious, who allows their life to be governed by fear, will find their world shrinking. Thus our freedom expands or contracts according to our choices. Free will is a matter of practice.

We can learn to take calculated risks: risks in the sense that we are prepared to venture beyond the conventional and the approval of others; but calculated in the sense that we think through the possible consequences of our actions and try to create a safety net if we can. We don't always need to jump off cliffs and hope for the best just to test out our faith in God's providence! Yet as we free ourselves from the constraints of our past and our fear of the unknown, the universe may open many possibilities that we can explore.

We may see our personal journeys taking place within the unfolding of a Great Plan designed by our Creator; or we may see ourselves making creative choices within a series of random events that comprise the evolution of our universe, governed only by immutable, anonymous laws. However we see the bigger picture, the journey that we make will be unique. No one will ever have a life quite like ours. No one will ever make the same contribution to the flow of the universe. No one can do exactly what we can do. We are in this sense our own creation, our own original work of art. It is an extraordinary feeling to realise quite how irreplaceable, how special we really are. What we must never lose sight of however is that we are all in this together. We don't have to like everyone on this planet but we need to recognise each other as fellow human beings. We travel together on this journey. We can learn from each other, we can learn to live together. Maybe one day we can learn to love each other. Or we can fight and scratch our way through history pretending to ourselves we are separate beings with no connection to each other – the choice is ours. What we can never do, however, is to be apart from each other at the deepest level. You and I are one another. We are one.

PART III:

WE CAN BUILD

HEAVEN ON EARTH

WE ARE THE SEEDS OF HEAVEN ON EARTH

Within each one of us is the seed of heaven on earth. We all have our own vision for the world that we would like to see. We may hope for a better future for humankind or simply to save the planet from its own destruction. Perhaps we sense a deep spiritual connection with all life which we have an urge to share. In whatever way we feel called, we look to find some way of realising our dream.

Yet the prospect of being able to do anything much about it can seem very daunting. The task may look so huge that it is all too easy to feel overwhelmed. We can feel very powerless in the face of all the forces that appear to be working against our ideals. It's enough to make anyone want to give up and understandably many people do.

But it would be a mistake. Each one of us has it within ourselves to grow the seed of heaven on earth. We can make the changes we need both for ourselves and the planet. We need simply to remember three key points:

- We need to work on ourselves if we want to be a force for good in the world.
- The work we do on ourselves will *of itself* have a positive influence on the planet.
- We have the resources to do this work. We are not being given an impossible task. In fact from a spiritual perspective we could say we are simply doing the work for which we have been sent. Individually and collectively we have all the support and resources we need. We just have to be willing to do the work.

WHAT IS TO BE DONE?

To understand why it is so important to work on ourselves if we want to create a better world we have only to look at some past attempts. Foremost amongst these in recent history has been the setting up of Communist systems during the 20th century, starting with the Russian revolution of 1917.

The mastermind behind this seizure of power was Vladimir Ilyich Ulyanov, better known as Lenin. In his early political development Lenin was deeply influenced by the works of the Russian radical Nikolai Chernyshevsky who wrote in 1863, "What To Do", a book about the life of a revolutionary and the struggle against the injustices of Tsarist Russia. Lenin became a Marxist and following in Chernyshevsky's footsteps wrote his own revolutionary manual in 1902 paraphrasing the title:

"What Is To Be Done."

This book laid the foundations of what was to become "Bolshevism", Lenin's own version of Marxism. It was his party, the Bolsheviks, who seized power in Russia in 1917 and attempted to create the world's first socialist state, the Union of Soviet Socialist Republics. Lenin was probably the most successful revolutionary of the modern age and the Communist organisation he set up spread to many parts of the world.

For a while it seemed to many to provide an answer to the ills of capitalism with its mass unemployment and ruthless exploitation of working people. But Lenin himself seems to have felt some frustration towards the end of his life about the pace and depth of change he had wrought in the Soviet Union. No matter how much energy he put into his work, no matter how many orders and exhortations he sent out, no matter even how many of his opponents he had imprisoned or executed, too many people seemed to cling on stubbornly to their old ways.

Worse still, under his successor Stalin, the brutal and authoritarian tendencies clearly in evidence under Lenin, became grotesquely caricatured into the hideous suffering and mass slaughter of Soviet citizens in the 1930s and 40s. This is not to deny the very real achievements of the Soviet Union. But to some extent they were despite rather than because of the Communist system. In the end this brave socialist experiment by most measures failed. It was characterised by appalling repression, a stagnating economy and a vast overblown bureaucracy unable or unwilling to reform itself. For all its claims of superiority, the USSR could not keep up with its Western capitalist rivals. The Soviet Union has disintegrated now, and most other Communist states have abandoned socialism in all but name. With the collapse of the Marxist ideal and the apparent triumph of global capitalism with its cold unrelenting economics, we may be left wondering if there really is another way to build a better society.

LESSONS OF GENIUS
AND STUPIDITY

Yet such a path does exist. How we get there, "What is to be done?" is the challenge for our generation. It is our opportunity to make our world vision come true, however unperfectly. We can learn from Lenin's life and revolutionary career, both in terms of what to avoid as well as what we can usefully build on. For Lenin exemplifies many of the strengths and weaknesses of those who have sought to change the world. In terms of political ability, Lenin exhibited real genius at times. But in his understanding of the nature of change and the work he needed to do he also exhibited the greatest stupidity. For he could not see the connection between what went on inside himself and the effect it had on the world outside. He believed he could change the world without changing himself and the result was by and large a disaster - and not just for him.

One way of understanding Lenin is to look at him from the point of view of the heart, mind and will, which symbolically speaking constitute the human condition[2]. From this perspective we can see there were imbalances in his life and work. Bolshevism if nothing else represents the triumph of the will: Lenin's will, in forging his organisation into a disciplined instrument; in deciding what course the revolution should take; and above all in enforcing his beliefs on the peoples of the Soviet Union. He was utterly dedicated, ruthless and single minded. In this he was aided by a first-class intellect and whilst he certainly made mistakes, in the pursuit of power most of his key political decisions were right. Lenin's weakness however lay in his disconnection from his heart. That is not to say he was the monster some anti-Communists have depicted him. There is plenty of evidence, particularly in his early years, of a warm, even gentle part of his being. But Lenin seems to have made an almost conscious decision to cut himself off from his more tender and compassionate feelings.

To gain some insight into this we can look back at events in his youth, which were to turn his world upside down. Lenin had an elder brother, Alexander, who he loved very much and looked up to when he was a boy. Once when he was young someone asked him what he wanted to be when he grew up. "I want to be like Alex" he replied. Unbeknownst to his family Alexander had joined a secret revolutionary organisation and had become

---

[2]To study further the source of the ideas behind this approach see Omraam Mikhaël Aïvanhov *Collected Works* and *Izvor Collection*

involved in a plot to assassinate the Tsar. He was caught by the authorities and condemned to death.

Lenin and his family were utterly devastated by the news. Lenin would avenge his brother's death and wage merciless war on the Russian government but perhaps significantly he took a different political path from Alexander. Maybe too at this point some cold steel entered his heart. It was almost as if the pain of his brother's death was too much to bear and he tried to bury his grief in his anger against the system. What we know for sure is that later on in his life when a friend played some beautiful classical music to him Lenin told him to stop, telling him that he could not do what he had to if he listened to such a moving piece. It was as if he had decided to disconnect from his heart in order to achieve his revolutionary goals.

But it was precisely this disconnection, this lack of compassion, that hardened his regime; that set up a new secret police; that built the first concentration camps; that closed down the opposition; that enforced all the harsh measures that have made his government infamous for its ruthlessness and brutality. The new Soviet society could not or would not free itself from its Tsarist inheritance so that in the end it became in many ways an imitation of the old repressive regime it had seemingly overthrown. The abused child of Tsarist Russia had become the Soviet abuser.

This failure reflected the inner process in Lenin: that he could not or would not heal the anger and the pain inside him. It was his inner state and that of all the other revolutionary leaders that were projected onto the wider political screen when the Bolsheviks became the new government. If people do not deal with their shadow side then no matter how good their conscious intentions they can create havoc if they achieve positions of power. Thus the noble ideal of freeing Russia from its Tsarist oppression was turned into the cold and repressive nightmare of Communist rule. This is not to say that the personal psychology of Lenin and his comrades is the only reason why the Soviet government was so harsh and authoritarian. But Lenin stamped his personality on his party and later on the Communist system that ran Russia so his inner torment had a direct and very destructive impact on the world around him.

So anyone involved in the process of world change needs to work on themselves. This is not a substitute for action but a complementary and parallel activity. We cannot create a united and peaceful society if we are at war within ourselves. We cannot liberate humanity if we have not freed ourselves from the inner demons that enslave us. We cannot bring love and justice to the world if there is none in our hearts. If we want to solve the world's problems we need to deal with our own too. This does not mean we have to become saints before we do anything about our planet. But it does mean that building heaven within ourselves needs to go hand in hand with building heaven in the outer world.

Section B

BUILDING A BETTER WORLD - STARTING WITH US

Building a better world may mean in the first instance focusing on our own growth and healing. There are many pathways. We may wish to use an established method, be it a spiritual discipline like Buddhism or one of the many forms of therapy. Sometimes the best approaches can be the ones we work out for ourselves. For we all have our own inner knowledge and resources that can guide us. A great deal can be done at little or no cost. For example:

- We may gain mutual support through the shared experience of a self-help group.
- We can experience the healing power of being in nature as well as using its remedies.
- We can use our thoughts creatively to change our outlook and visualise a positive future for ourselves and the world.

The key is willingness. We have the power to heal something in our lives no matter how many problems we think we have. Whatever challenges we face we can be sure that we, like the rest of the world, only have them because they *can* be healed. There will always be a path that will take us through the difficulties we encounter however daunting they may seem. But we will need the willingness to take that first step. It could be admitting something to ourselves or asking for help or deciding to stop putting off dealing with a problem. Whatever that first step is, only we can do it. No matter what help is available, no matter how much knowledge or good advice we have, it will always be we who have to take responsibility for our lives.

Of course we have the choice to stay locked into our problems, going round and round in circles, bemoaning our lot without really being prepared to do anything much about it. We can tell ourselves we *can't* change when really we mean *won't*. Wanting always to be the victim, we can become attached to our suffering. For each of us there may be a time of great pain in our lives where we experience our own sense of crucifixion. Yet if we do not work through this there is the danger that the cross becomes oddly comfortable and we develop a kind of "crucifixion addiction". It is not that the pain in our lives has not been real. It's just that there comes a time when we need to get off the cross.

We can decide to move on and change the way we look at our lives. We can gradually learn to turn the traumas and hurt we may have experienced to our advantage. Even in the most difficult situation we can ask ourselves, "What is the gift in this for me?" or "What is the universe trying to teach me?". We should never be afraid to ask others for help and to draw upon their wisdom and experience to encourage us and illuminate our path. What we should not expect (or allow) is for others to do our own work for us. Nor should we assume that what worked for one person is going to work in precisely the same way (if at all) for us.

We may need to deal with our past. The experiences we have as we are growing up can affect us very deeply but we do not have to become prisoners of our childhood traumas. We have the power to change the patterns of thought and feeling that we have developed over the years with honesty, self-awareness and a willingness to work on ourselves. One of the things that can be helpful for us to examine is the extent to which our lives have been a self-fulfilling prophecy. In our early years we can develop views - about life, about ourselves, about men and women, about people in authority for example - without us noticing it.

These can become a kind of prophecy, one that life will always seem to fulfil. For instance if we believe we can trust no one, then we may well find ourselves constantly let down. Every time it happens, it seems to confirm our original negative view. Contradictory experiences are discounted. It may be that we attract people into our lives that will fulfil our pessimistic outlook. It may be we subconsciously create situations where we feel betrayed. We can repeat old patterns that no longer help us and are even destructive to ourselves or others. But if we bring these into awareness we can begin to free ourselves from their baleful hidden influence on our lives. Like Hercules and the Hydra we can lift up our "monsters" out of the darkness of the swamp of unconsciousness and hold it in the light where they lose their power and can be healed.

Each one of us can create something wonderful out of our lives. But if our will is under the control of an addiction or compulsion, it will restrict our ability to pursue our chosen path and be of help to the world or ourselves. Sometimes because our addiction does not appear severe or life threatening to us, we can fool ourselves into thinking that somehow we don't really have a problem that needs dealing with. But addictive traits can be very pernicious in their effects and it can only benefit us if we face our inner demons. There are self-help groups and other ways open to us to free ourselves from the grip of these addictions and compulsions.

As we emerge from the influence of these destructive patterns we may come to trust the healing process we are in. Gradually we sense new possibilities opening up for us in life. We may come to feel that our liberation from the shadow of addiction and compulsion is for a higher purpose. It is as if all we had been through was a preparation for the work that we feel inspired to do not just for ourselves but for all humanity. Spiritually we may feel that we are being guided towards our highest destiny.

A FEELING INSIDE

Most important in all this - and sometimes most difficult - is the need to forgive, not least ourselves. Forgiveness is not about condoning behaviour or saying something does not matter. Forgiving is letting go. It lets us dump all the old baggage that we may have been carrying around for years, all the bitterness and resentment and hurt and pain that can cast a shadow over our lives. Forgiveness is a gift to ourselves. If someone has wronged us it enables us to be inwardly free of them. It does not mean they should not be held to account if justice demands it or wisdom suggests it. But it would be without rancour or desire for revenge.

It can be helpful in our daily lives, particularly when times seem hard, to remember all the things that we can feel grateful for. It can be as simple as having shelter for the night or the beauty of nature or the kindness of a stranger. The more we can focus on the positive things in our lives the more we will attract these things to us. That does not mean we ignore or suppress our problems. But we can see them as opportunities to provide valuable lessons for us and thus turn them to our advantage.

This is the true alchemy – transforming life's leaden experiences into the gold of growth and enlightenment. In time then we can see what appear to be negative elements in our lives actually to be positive ones in disguise. In reality we are in a win–win situation: everything in life either is, or can be turned to, good - if we have the mind to do it. It's a matter of how we choose to make use of our experiences. Building heaven on earth is much about realising it is already here.

Throughout life we will go through ups and downs, big and small. For most of us, it will affect how we feel. Imagine we've seen a wonderful film. We come out of the cinema with our partner and we're feeling great. Then as we walk home, a car passes and splashes us with mud. Or maybe a drunken person staggering by hurls some abuse at us. Now we are angry and upset. What all these changes in mood have in common is that they are influenced by external events. Looked at this way, our happiness seems to be at the mercy of forces beyond our control. But it doesn't have to be like that. We can decide not to let an unfortunate episode ruin our entire evening. We can make emotional choices just as we can make intellectual ones, though it may take practice.

If we go yet more deeply into our own being we will discover our natural state of joy. Regardless of the difficulties we are going through, there is something within us that just shines. We could say from a spiritual perspective it radiates from the soul. But whatever its origin, it exists quite independently of outside circumstances. Thus we can feel joyful and sad at the same time. One comes from the depth of our being and at some level is telling us everything is OK; the other is our natural human reaction to a loss or hurt. As we become more aware of the joy that is always with us, we can begin to let go of our attachment to the moments of happiness that will inevitably come and go in our lives. We no longer need to try to fix our feelings with drink or drugs or constant distractions. Humans may seek happiness but joy just *is*. Even if we can't feel it right now we can know that it is shining inside us. In awakening to this inner truth we take an important step in setting our hearts free to create a new world, within and without.

BEING ONE BEING

Letting go of the hurt and pain of the past we can move on to where we are right now. We can begin by embracing the oneness of ourselves. We have already seen the importance of accepting all parts of our psyche, both shadow and light. Just as the peoples of the world can come together as one, so we can integrate all parts of our being - body, mind, heart and soul - into a unity.

Here we may face challenges from our cultural inheritance. In the West there has been an ascetic tradition that pitted spirit against matter, body against soul. Its followers have seen the body and its needs as an impediment to spiritual growth. In the belief that they were serving God, they neglected their physical well being and turned their back on the world. In so doing they created a duality between body and spirit that resulted in great imbalances, whatever their good intentions. They cut themselves off from the vital energies of life rather than embracing them as part of God's Creation. In modern times echoes of this are to be found amongst some scholars who focus almost exclusively on the intellect which is seen as the pinnacle of human achievement. In so doing the needs of the hearts and the body can be neglected so that they cannot really connect with other people or even themselves. So as we seek to build a new future it is important that we bring our awareness into our hearts and bodies, our minds and souls, honouring them as vital parts of who we are on this planet. It is thus within ourselves that our sense of oneness can take root.

As we grow in strength and confidence we can take our spirituality and our ideas into the market place and integrate them with our daily lives. There may also be times when we need to withdraw from the hustle and bustle of the outside world, finding stillness be it in meditation or in a quiet place. It is important to find space for ourselves to recharge our batteries and seek our own sense of inner connection. But this is a means to an end not an end in itself. We really are meant to be here on earth.

Being in touch with all the aspects of our nature - physical, emotional, mental and spiritual - means we also can avoid leaving parts of our being behind as we progress through life.

For if our mind decides on a course of action without regard to our emotional or physical needs, we can find ourselves zooming off into the distance dragging our poor body behind or neglecting our feelings. Sooner or later our physical or emotional health will suffer. Alternatively if our heart alone determines our actions we can become dominated by our emotions and embark on schemes that have not been thought through. Disaster ensues and we are left wondering why it all went wrong when we meant to do so much good. Perhaps we are driven by great ambition but because we lack wisdom and compassion we cause great misery and destruction as we career through life like a runaway bulldozer. If our sexuality is not connected to our heart it can become cold and loveless; if we do not use our wisdom we can end up in all sorts of foolishness and danger.

Embracing all the parts of our being is thus a key element in maintaining our sense of oneness as we evolve. We can learn to listen within and respond to the ebb and flow of our own inner rhythms and the currents of life around us. We need neither drag our feet nor rush ahead of ourselves. Rather we can grow and develop as a whole human being at our own natural pace. In this spirit we can explore the richness of our hearts, our minds and our bodies. Each one offers us many gifts if we are willing to go beyond the confines of the conventional view of them.

By the same token we need not limit ourselves in how we develop our senses. In the industrialised world great store is set on the intellect, which is sometimes seen as being synonymous with intelligence. Whilst the intellect certainly has its uses and can be a marvellous tool for the right purposes, it is not the only faculty we possess. There are other senses we can use. Our intuition can work with great speed and accuracy to guide us to a solution rather than spending hours on supposedly rational calculations that can so easily miss the mark. Intuition also has a way of sensing the whole picture rather than just analysing a particular fragment of it. We can learn to tune in to a scenario and listen within so that we can reach a deeper understanding than can normally be achieved by using the intellect on its own. We can also gradually learn to discern the true voice of intuition distinct from other senses such as instinct. Instinct, which derives from our animal nature, also can be useful. But it is not as refined or holistic as intuition. It deals with the basics of survival. Intuition takes us much further. This is a process that takes time and practice. But the more we explore our inner senses the greater our capacity to sense inwardly our path to realising our vision of heaven on earth.

Developing our personal sense of oneness allows us to embrace the diversity of our bodies. In many cultures there is an idealised image of what the body should be like. It might be about the overall shape or weight of the body; the size of breasts or the length of the penis; it may be the colour of the hair or skin. It can change over time. But it is astonishing how powerful these ideas are. We can absorb them in conversation or through the media without really noticing. Yet like all forms of prejudice their effect can be extremely damaging. People's lives can be turned into a misery because they feel they don't fit the mould. The pressure to conform to a conventional body image can feel overwhelming. No wonder this mentality is sometimes referred to as "body fascism".

But we don't need to accept it. Challenging stereotypes can be part of accepting ourselves fully as we are. It is entirely subjective what constitutes "handsome" or "beautiful" or "sexy" and no one has the right to determine what someone should or shouldn't look like. This does not mean we can't alter our bodies to suit our needs. We may choose to gain or lose weight for reasons of health or comfort. A surgical intervention may be necessary or desirable in some circumstances. We may choose to decorate or change our body in some way to enhance its beauty in our eyes. But we need not feel that we have to conform to other people's preferences or rigid conventions in how we look.

The issue of conformity and diversity does not only apply to our bodies. Bringing heart, mind, body and soul together we can create a wonderful mix of shapes, sizes and abilities. This diversity should be a cause for human celebration: it is an expression of the creative freedom of our evolution. Being different, whether genetically or socially, gives us the room to explore and experiment which is essential for our development as a species. Yet whether it be our physical appearance, our views or lifestyle there has been a tendency for people to feel that everyone has to fit in to a preordained mould. This has gone on for centuries but its most horrific manifestation in recent times was Nazism. This ideology created in people a picture of the "perfect" racial specimen and sought to eliminate all those who didn't fit in. Their list included all those who were differently abled physically or mentally; lesbian or gay or transgender people; gypsies and other members of the so-called "inferior" races and above all the Jews. They claimed they were threats to the "purity" of their race. And they so sought to exterminate them all in the pursuit of their "perfection".

With the defeat of Nazism in 1945, when the horrors of the camps were exposed, it might have been hoped that their philosophy would have been thoroughly discredited. Yet there are still echoes of this ideology clinging on here and there and even finding new forms as technology opens all sorts of avenues for human engineering. For example it is present in the idea that it is morally acceptable to abort foetuses solely on the grounds that they are likely to be born physically or mentally handicapped. Or the plan to create "designer" babies with all their "imperfections" removed so that they will conform to the prejudices of the age. This mentality comes from the greatest ignorance, both scientifically and spiritually, about how the universe works. Evolutionary quirkiness is a natural and essential part of Creation. Humans seek conformity but nature loves diversity. We are all part of the Oneness and each one of us has the right to be here in whatever form or shape we appear on this planet.

THE PATH TO BUILDING HEAVEN ON EARTH

As we grow through life we may reach a point when we choose to make a commitment to follow its course wherever it may take us. There are many ways of understanding this: we could say we are doing the work our heart most yearns for; or we may see it as fulfilling our soul purpose. As we go more deeply into this process we gradually find our will, our entire being, becomes lined up with that which is most loving, most noble, most pure within our own sense of oneness. This is when we enter a state of "spiritual alignment". In a secular sense we could say it is when we consecrate our lives to the highest ideals. Religiously it is expressed beautifully and simply by the single word "Islam". Islam means to submit, to submit to the will of God. We could say we must all become Moslems in this inner sense to carry out this great work for humanity. Equally we could see it as opening ourselves up to be guided by our connection with the universe. In the end all roads lead to oneness.

It is not to be supposed that this process is always an easy one. There are many obstacles to overcome and we may experience times when we seem to lose all sense of purpose or even meaning. This is 'the dark night of the soul' and if we pass through it, we can be sure we are on the right road, strange as that may feel at the time. Yet by pursuing this path, we can achieve what might otherwise remain only a dream. We can let our light shine and in so doing encourage others in their work. For we have the power to change the world.

Section C

WE HAVE THE POWER
TO CHANGE THE WORLD

As we begin to build heaven on earth we begin to realise the power each one of us has. For the work we do on ourselves has an impact that goes far beyond those immediately around us. Because we are all connected the way we live forms part of the changes that affect our planet. Our thoughts, feelings and actions have their own power. We can sense this in places where people pray or meditate regularly when we can often feel a very peaceful and uplifting atmosphere. Similarly in places where terrible things have happened traces can also be left and people who are sensitive enough will pick this up. But this is not only true of particular places - it is true of the whole planet.

Thus it is that our own personal healing can bring a healing to the world. Through what we think, say and do as we go about our daily lives, each one of us is subtly contributing to the planetary atmosphere. When we work on ourselves, we can spread love and goodness on a global scale with our positive thoughts and feelings. As we transform the pain and hurt in our lives into a deeper understanding and compassion, so the energy we create can go to help someone else in their journey wherever they are in the world.

In truth the global impact of how we live our lives is beyond imagination. Each one of us can create a little bit of heaven on earth, within and without, through the work we do each day. If we clean just one bowl with love and care and reverence we create a tiny atmosphere of such beauty that its power spreads across the world so that somewhere a life is uplifted, a distressed soul is calmed, a gentleness is brought to an angry mind. This is the power we have been given, the power to change the world. It is given to each one of us, no matter how poor or insignificant we think we are. With it comes a great responsibility. But know that we are not helpless. We are not victims. We are not mere cogs in a machine. We, the people of this planet, have the power.

Collectively the impact of our thoughts and feelings on the world is extraordinary. In recent years there have been some remarkable changes in the attitudes of political leaders that have been influenced by positive shifts in global consciousness. Both the dismantling of the apartheid system in South Africa and the collapse of the Soviet Empire are not entirely explicable in purely material terms. It is true that both regimes were under economic and political pressure but in both cases their leaders could have carried on trying to preserve their systems of government. Yet both Gorbachev in the USSR and de Klerk in South Africa decided to do the unthinkable and let go of power.

WORKING WITH WISDOM
AND COMPASSION

From the person who tends their garden with thought and care to the activist who campaigns for world justice - all have something to important to contribute. We each have an opportunity to make something astonishing and unique, of such splendour and grace from the raw materials of our being. It is as if there was a gigantic quilt stretching across the universe made from the quintessence of all our lives. Imagine that for each one of us there is a patch bounded neither by time or space that we are free to work on. We can create whatever colours or patterns, use whatever fabrics or shapes we will, yet our work forms part of an infinitely greater whole. It is in this way that we need both a clear sense of personal boundaries as well as knowing we are all interconnected. The work we do will benefit the rest of the world but we also can respect each individual's right and responsibility to create their own part of the quilt.

So if we choose to work for global change by becoming directly involved in other people's lives we need to work with wisdom as well as compassion. When trying to help people with their problems we can act with awareness so we do not disempower those whom we seek to support by presuming to know all the answers and trying to control their lives. Thus in our compassion we are appalled by child labour but in our wisdom we know we must think through how something better might be put in its place that supports the child and replaces the lost income.

It is also important to be clear about our own motives. If our involvement is born out of a superficial emotional response it may not last. Weeping buckets of tears does not feed a hungry child or build a hospital. It is also very hard to be truly helpful to people or causes if we have too many attachments, either to them or to the outcome of the project we are involved with. This is particularly important for the kind of world work we may be participating in for the results may not be obvious or immediate. It may be easier to be genuinely helpful if we can develop an attitude of *loving detachment*, that is being motivated by a sense of deep compassion without getting hooked into the drama of other people's lives or the need for public recognition of our work.

There are also useful lessons in wisdom and compassion from the past. One cautionary tale comes from Lenin's decision to follow the path of violence. It was not a particularly surprising decision - he was brought up in an authoritarian system that repressed dissent with great brutality - but it was not a wise one.

It seemed to offer the only way to change the Tsarist regime and it certainly worked in the narrow sense of helping him get to power. But it ultimately corrupted the ideals for which he fought. He began to rely more and more on force rather than argument and persuasion to get his way and the system he created increasingly echoed the harsh repression of the old order that had been supposedly overthrown. And his methods attracted people who were drawn to violence for its own sake. As often happens in organisations that use force, violence becomes an end rather than just a means.

On the other hand one of Lenin's successes was his decision to build up his forces *outside* the existing power structures and instead focus on providing an alternative government (in his case making use of worker and peasant councils or Soviets). Other political parties allowed themselves to be sucked into the system and ultimately became compromised and discredited. What worked to Lenin's political advantage may have a more general relevance to us as we seek to build a better world. We can of course try to change things from within but there are clear dangers to this, as Lenin's rivals discovered to their cost.

That does not mean we should not take advantage of the opportunities for change that the system allows us – for instance it is important to use our vote wherever we can. But in general it may be better to focus our energies on providing clear alternatives. We have to demonstrate, albeit within the constraints of the existing order, that there are better ways of doing things, of resolving issues, of organising our lives than the current system.

And for this there are many encouraging signs. Across the world people are coming together in different ways to find new ways to deal with old problems. Over the last 50 years or so, for instance, there has been a mushrooming of self-help groups.

Many different kinds of healing are being developed to help us with our physical, emotional, mental and spiritual diseases. Worldwide over 175 million people belong to co-operatives. Not-for-profit companies provide another alternative to the exploitative free-market capitalist model. So much good is going on in the world.

New currents are flowing across this planet and today we have the chance to unfurl our sails and catch the wind that will take us to the new world we are seeking. We are passing through a time of extremely rapid change and great turbulence as we undergo a great planetary healing. For now it may sometimes be wise to experiment with new forms and structures that do not require massive investments of time and energy or we may become bogged down in the dead weight of institutional inertia. Organisationally speaking we do not always need to build great cathedrals, which take decades to set up and are hard to change, impressive and beautiful as they are. We can do as nomadic Mongols do and figuratively speaking build tents that are easy to put up and take down. In this way we can adapt and grow rapidly in what is for the moment a fluid situation.

OUR CHALLENGE

Courage, Maya Angelou once said, was the most important virtue of them all for without it none of the others could manifest. And to participate in this great world awakening to the Oneness we will all need courage. Courage can take many forms. There is the heroic courage of those who die for their beliefs. There is the quiet courage of millions of ordinary people who get up every day and deal with life's tasks as best they can with little outward recognition or reward. Then there is another kind of courage, the courage to be who you really are. It is the courage of the transsexual, to assert an inner truth of being whatever the world is telling you, whatever the obstacles. It is this courage in particular that is so important in bringing a healing to the world.

People who are not afraid to be who they are have a special aura about them that can awaken the same sense of freedom in those whose lives they touch. Whatever is inside us - our hopes our vision, our sense of spirituality - needs to shine through if we are to realise our true potential, or, from another perspective, if we are to fulfil God's plan for us. We have the chance during our lives to let go of our fears and be true to ourselves. But this is something we can do gradually, step by step. Courage can be a matter of practice. Not all of us are born heroes!

And yet every moment of our lives does matter. What we do counts. Raising our kids is as important a task for the future of the world as signing a disarmament treaty. Do not be fooled into thinking that because we don't see the results of something splashed across the front page of a newspaper somehow it isn't significant. Each act is a tiny droplet but together they are a mighty ocean. As the movement for world unity gathers momentum, we will reach a 'critical mass' when the whole of society will shift decisively in favour of the universal principle that *we are one*. But we must not leave this work to others. For two thousand years Christians have been reciting the words of Jesus' prayer:

Thy will be done
On earth as it is in heaven

But - Christian or not - we need to make it happen. Are we going to sit there, waiting, expecting God or some world leader to do all the work for us? The Universe will help us, we are being helped now, we are being guided and encouraged. But we have our part to play as well. Heaven and earth is a co-operative too! *We* can build the 'New Jerusalem' in partnership with our higher source, however we understand it.

So this is the challenge we can set ourselves: I dare you to believe we can make this world one. I dare you to realise you make a difference. I dare you to see the vision and begin the journey that will make it real. I dare you to feel your own freedom and empowerment and participate in this glorious work for all humanity. I dare you to allow yourself to make mistakes, to learn and grow and build something truly marvellous. I dare you to reach your Promised Land and to live it every day of your life. I dare you to be who you really are.

I dare you.

The Five Principles
Of Universal Humanity

1. *We recognise humanity as one family and we acknowledge that our loyalty to our humanity transcends all others such as those of nationality, race or religion.*

2. *We accept every part of ourselves as we grow and learn both as individuals and communities, excluding none from the possibility of change and redemption.*

3. *We embrace our oneness with nature with reverence and respect for all life.*

4. *We affirm the fundamental equality, dignity and value of each one of us and seek to end forever the exploitation of one human being by another.*

5. *We respect the liberty of each individual, conscious that as children of one universe our fates are indissolubly bound together.*

About the author

Simenon Honoré was born in Oxford, England in 1952. Graduating in History from London University's School of Slavonic and East European Studies, Simenon spent over 25 years as a teacher of History, Politics and meditation. He has been involved in both political and spiritual movements as well as working through his own personal healing. Simenon has published a number of articles and books including co-authoring a recovery text for addicts. He has also been involved in setting up self-help groups and has given talks on personal and planetary change within the overall theme of human spirituality.